Decoding the Golf Ball Flight

Decoding the Golf Ball Flight

The Art of Shotmaking

First Edition

XICHAO MO

PACLINX PUBLISHING

DECODING THE GOLF BALL FLIGHT

COPYRIGHT ©2019, XICHAO MO

All rights reserved.

No part of this book may be reproduced or transmitted in any form or by any means, electronic or mechanical, or stored in any information storage and retrieval systems, without the prior written permission of the publisher.

FIRST EDITION

OCTOBER, 2019

ISBN-13: 978-1-7333154-0-1
ISBN-10: 1-7333154-0-3

Paclinx

PUBLISHED BY PACLINX CORPORATION

Books published by Paclinx Corporation are available at special quality discounts for education, training, and other programs. For more information, please visit www.paclinx.com.

Golf is a Thinker's Game

CONTENTS

ACKNOWLEDGEMENTS XI

INTRODUCTION XIII

1. **BALL FLIGHT LAWS** 1

   A Game of Control 1
   The Power of Knowledge 2
   The Evolution of Ball Flight Laws 3
   Ball Flight Patterns 3
   Three Ball Flight Shapes 4
   Three Launch Directions 6
   Nine Ball Flight Patterns 7

2. **GOLF BALL AND THE AIR** 9

   What Is So Special about Golf? 10
   Spin 11
   The Magnus Effect 12
   Direction of the Magnus force 14
   Drag Reduction 15
   Tilted Spin Axis 16
   Summary 18

3. **DIVIDE AND CONQUER** 19

   Vector and Scalar 19
   Vector Composition 20
   Vector Decomposition 21

4. **SPIN AND IMPACT** 26

   Perpendicular Collision 26
   Oblique Collision 29
   Impact Analysis 29
   Launch Vector VL 31

v

Spinning Vector VS	31
Spin Experiments	33
Spin Rate and Ball Speed	34

5. STRAIGHT SHOTS 36

Keep it Square	36
Y-plane	37
Square to Swing Direction	38
Neutral Shaft Position	39
Club Loft	39
Effective Loft	40
Spin Loft	41
Angle of Attack	42
How They Are Related	43
Clubhead Velocity at Impact	43
The Important Equations for Ball Flight	46
Launch Angle	48
Spin vs. Club Loft	51
Backspin: an Indispensable Element in Golf	52
How to Boost Backspin	53
Launch Angle vs. Distance	53
Distance Gap	55

6. CURVE SHOTS 56

Non-square Strikes	56
Open-face Strike	57
The Attributes of a Fade Shot	58
How to Hit a Fade	58
How to Fix a Slice	60
Closed-face Strike	63
The Attributes of a Draw Shot	65
How to Hit a Draw	65
Launch Direction	66
Spin Axis	69
Why Is It Much Easier to Slice with Drivers?	71
Ball Flight Summary	72

7. D-PLANE 75
What on earth is this D-plane? 75
D-plane in a Square Strike 76
D-plane in a Non-square Strike 78
The Essence of D-plane 80
Summary 82

8. SOLID CONTACT 83
The Importance of Making Solid Contact 84
Where is the Sweet Spot? 84
Making Solid Contact with an Iron 86
Making Solid Contact with a Driver 90
Smash Factor 91
Checking Impact Locations Regularly 92

9. OFF-CENTER IMPACT 94
Off-center Shots 94
Moment of Inertia (MOI) 96
Gear Effect for Woods 97
Gear Effect for Irons 99
Bulge 100
Roll 101
Dealing with Gear Effects 102
Gear Effect Examples 102

10. GOLF BALLS 106
Golf Ball Specifications 106
Ball Construction 108
Cover Materials 110
Dimples 111
Compression 113
Choosing the Right Balls 114

11. GROOVES AND SPIN 115
Grooves Matter? 115
The Groove Controversy 116
The USGA's Groove Study 118

The USGA's Key Findings on Grooves 119
The New Groove Rules 121
Keep the Grooves Clean and Fresh 122
Grooves on a Driver 123

12. IRON SWING VS. DRIVER SWING **125**

The Iron Swing 125
The Driver Swing 131

GLOSSARY **137**

Angle of Attack 137
Ball Speed 137
Carry Distance 138
Clubhead Speed 138
COR 138
Dynamic Loft 139
Effective Loft 139
Face Angle 139
Draw 140
Fade 140
Face-to-Path 140
Hook 141
Horizontal Launch Angle 141
Horizontal Swing Direction 141
Landing Angle 141
Launch Angle 142
Launch Direction 142
Launch Monitor 143
Launch vector 143
Moment of Inertia, MOI 143
Offset Distance 143
Pull 144
Push 144
Neutral Shaft Position 144
Slice 144
Smash Factor 144
Spin Axis 145

Spinning Vector 145
Spin Loft 145
Spin Rate 146
Striking Plane 146
Swing Path 146
Swing Direction 147
Swing Plane Angle 147
Target Line 147
Total Distance 147
Vertical Launch Angle 148
Y-plane 148

ABOUT THE AUTHOR **149**

Acknowledgements

I would like to extend my sincere appreciation to all the people who offered their support and assistance to the publication of this book:

Dr. Heng Zhao, Neil Gayle, Jian Sun, and Bryce Barbato for their technical review and detailed comments on the book's structure and readability.

Ms. Roginsky for her editing and proofreading of the non-technical contents of the manuscript.

Mr. Hall, Adam Novak, Jim Brosnahan, Andrew Arbesfeld, Curtis Metcalf, Sarah Xia, Cynthia Mo, and Derek Mo for their valuable feedback and constructive suggestions.

Cynthia Mo for modeling.

Maria Hazinas for contributing to the graphic design.

INTRODUCTION

During the first two years of my golf journey, I noticed that the little ball seemed to have a mind of its own. Instead of going straight to the target I chose, it would often make an unexpected right turn and end up in a water hazard. My fellow golfers told me that was a slice. Not knowing what was causing those ugly slices, I became very frustrated. At one point, I developed a fear of tee shots. The first corrective action I took to address this terrifying issue was spending 300 dollars on a brand new TaylorMade driver, which helped but didn't fix the problem.

The instructor I sought help from merely told me to hold the club using a stronger grip. Somehow I felt that wasn't the root cause of my problem and didn't want to commit to a "Band-Aid" solution. I suspected something else in my swing needed fixing.

During that time, I bought a training aid called Swing Groover, which was basically a golf ball attached to an L-shaped metal bracket through a nylon rope. A golfer would hit the ball, and then judge the clubhead swing path by how the ball rotates around the pivot. This training aid came with a one-page instruction sheet that briefly described how swing path and clubface orientation influenced ball flights. That sheet of paper became my first lesson on ball flight and inspired me to look deeper into this fascinating subject.

I soon discovered that ball flight laws were not as difficult as I had imagined. With the help of basic physics and a simple analytical technique called vector decomposition, I soon had a much better understanding of the ball-club interaction.

As a side note, I ultimately figured out why beginners tend to hit slices and published my findings in *Decoding the Golf Swing Plane*, which became one of the bestselling golf books on Amazon.

The knowledge of ball flight laws allowed me to quickly improve my ball striking skills and it also made practice much more effective and enjoyable. Within a couple of weeks, I was able to get my slicing under control. I also had a lot of fun in learning to shape shots. It was a great feeling to be able to diagnose ball flight issues on the spot and make swing adjustments all by myself.

I wished I had acquired the knowledge of ball flight much sooner. That certainly would have made learning the game less frustrating. A good understanding of ball flight will undoubtedly make life easier for average golfers. Unfortunately, the information on this topic hasn't been presented systematically and consistently in existing publications. The goal of this book is to make the essential pieces of golf ball flight available in one place so average golfers can become familiar with this subject early on in their golfing journey. The information in this book will also help advanced players and teaching professionals consolidate their knowledge of golf ball flight using a scientific approach.

1. Ball Flight Laws

How can I hit shots that are far and straight?
How do I get my approach shots to stick on the green?
Why do beginners tend to slice but rarely hook?
Why are my shots flying too high?

To answer these questions, golfers must understand how a golf ball interacts with the clubhead and how it behaves in the air. In the golf community, the rules describing such interactions and behaviors are called the *Ball Flight Laws*.

A Game of Control

Golf is a game of control. A player's ultimate goal is to deliver the ball to an intended target by controlling the direction, distance, and trajectory of each shot. When we have proper control over the little ball, the game is fun, rewarding, and even addictive. Here is how golf legend Ben Hogan put it in his famous book *Five Lessons*:

"One of the greatest pleasures in golf — I can think of nothing that truly compares with it unless it is watching a well-played shot streak for the flag — is the sensation a golfer experiences at the instant he contacts the ball flush and correctly. He always knows when he does, for then and only then does a distinctive 'sweet feeling' sweep straight up the shaft from the clubhead and surge through his arms and his whole frame."

A great number of amateur golfers, especially those who have never broken 90, probably have not experienced the "sweet feeling" Ben Hogan described. A big part of the problem, from what I have observed, is the lack of systematic knowledge on ball flight and ball striking among average golfers.

It is true that nowadays the almighty internet offers plenty of information on golf ball flight and ball striking, and dedicated golfers can always dig out something here or there. Yet locating the relevant data can often be a time-consuming process. When facing a variety of opinions, it is also a challenging task to separate the wheat from the chaff. Unfortunately, this is what most average golfers are dealing with these days.

THE POWER OF KNOWLEDGE

Mastering the knowledge of ball flight will be a turning point for anyone's golf game, as it was for mine. The fear of slice had troubled me for a long time before I finally have a good understanding of ball flight and swing plane. After learning how a ball would interact with a club, I was able to make swing adjustments and hit straight drives within two weeks. The slice might still come back for a visit occasionally, but I would no longer panic because now I know how to deal with it.

I had also struggled with my irons and was unable to hit solid and penetrating shots. Within a month, the knowledge of ball flight and ball striking enabled me to produce my first pure iron shot, which left behind a beautiful target-side divot and a pleasant sensation. It was a moment I would never forget! I still remember the amazing shockwave that arrived at my hands through the shaft. That must have been the "sweet feeling" Ben Hogan mentioned.

I really wish someone had given me a thorough lesson on ball flight, ball striking, and swing plane in my first year of learning golf. Given that, I certainly would have made much quicker progress and enjoyed the game much more.

Golf is also known as a game of misses. Even the best players in the world will inevitably hit bad shots or experience difficulties from time to time. When things go wrong, knowledge of ball flight allows a golfer to think clearly, diagnose the problem correctly, and find solutions quickly.

In addition, ball flight knowledge will make it easier for golfers to put together the pieces of the golf puzzle, which all exist in harmony as you will eventually find out.

The Evolution of Ball Flight Laws

In the old days, it was a common belief among golfers that a ball's initial launch direction was mainly determined by the clubhead's moving direction (often referred to as the swing path) right before impact. This claim was part of the so-called "old ball flight laws."

With the advent of high-speed video cameras and advanced launch monitors, people have been able to measure and record ball flight data and soon realized the "old ball flight laws" were not correct. Now we are in the era of "new ball flight laws," which depict that a ball's initial launch direction is predominantly determined by the clubface orientation instead of the swing path. However, the influence of the "old ball flight laws" doesn't go away completely, and its presence can still be seen on the internet.

The golf industry has contributed the discovery of the "new ball flight laws" to the advent of advanced launch monitors, especially the Trackman. The way I see it, the truth could have been easily revealed by seeking guidance from the basic principles of physics.

In the following chapters, we will introduce a simple analytical tool called *vector decomposition*, which will help golfers thoroughly understand the golf impact process without relying on expensive instruments.

Ball Flight Patterns

A specific golf ball flight pattern is the result of a particular ball-club collision, which happens so fast that its details easily elude our naked eyes. Only sophisticated high-speed video cameras, which are capable of recording thousands of frames per second, can show us exactly what happens at impact.

Fortunately, a ball's trajectory in the air can shed light on how it is struck and will give golfers the crucial feedback needed for swing adjustment. For this reason, the ability to identify typical ball flight patterns and determine their probable causes is a valuable skill for any golfer who wants to improve his game.

THREE BALL FLIGHT SHAPES

While traveling in the air, a ball takes a particular shape of trajectory, which is determined by the ball properties, the impact attributes, gravity, and various aerodynamic forces. Essentially, there are three basic ball flight shapes in golf, as shown in Fig. 1-1.

- Straight
- Fade
- Draw

First, let's get one thing "straight." In golf, a straight shot doesn't mean its trajectory in the three-dimensional space is a straight line, which is not possible due to the action of gravity. It simply means that a ball's flight path stays within a vertical plane and the ball travels to its destination without curving left or right. Or we can say the path's projection on the ground appears to be a straight line.

A fade is a shot that curves in the direction of a player's dominant hand as he faces the target. For right-handed golfers, a fade refers to a ball trajectory that curves from left to right. Some tour players, such as Tiger Woods, like to call it a cut. A ball flight curving severely in this direction is called a slice, which is the type of shot that often ends up in a water hazard, woods, or someone's backyard.

A draw is a shot that curves in the opposite direction of a golfer's dominant hand. For right-handed golfers, it refers to a trajectory that curves from right to left. A ball flight with a severe curvature in this direction is called a hook, which is a problem often experienced by better players.

Since ball flight shapes are defined from a player's perspective, they are just the opposite for left-handed golfers. For them, a fade curves left and a draw turns right. For the sake of conciseness, the discussions in this book are based on the perspective of right-handed golfers unless stated otherwise.

Ball Flight Laws

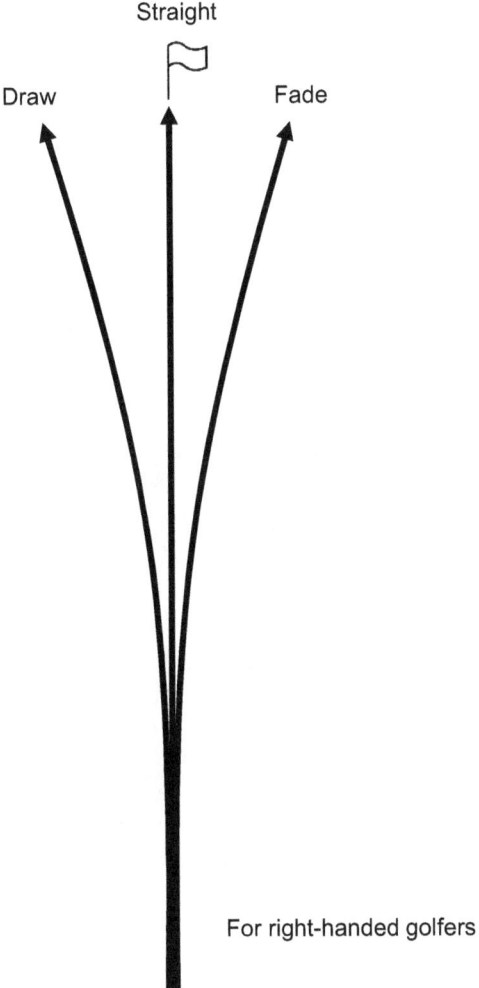

Fig. 1-1 Three Ball Flight Shapes

THREE LAUNCH DIRECTIONS

A ball flight also has three possible initial launch directions: *centered, push, and pull*. Just like draw and fade, push and pull are also defined from the player's perspective. For right-handed golfers, a push is a shot that launches straight towards the right of the intended target, whereas a pull is one that goes straight towards the left side (Fig. 1-2). For left-handed golfers, the definitions for push and pull are just the opposite.

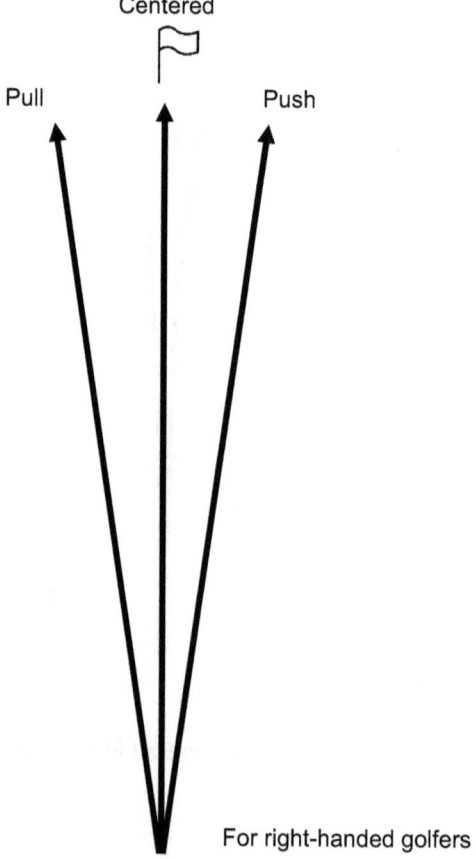

Fig. 1-2 Three Launch Directions

Nine Ball Flight Patterns

Together, the trajectory shapes and launch directions create nine possible combinations, which are known as the *nine ball flight patterns* (Fig. 1-3). For simplicity, the diagram only shows patterns from a right-handed golfer's perspective.

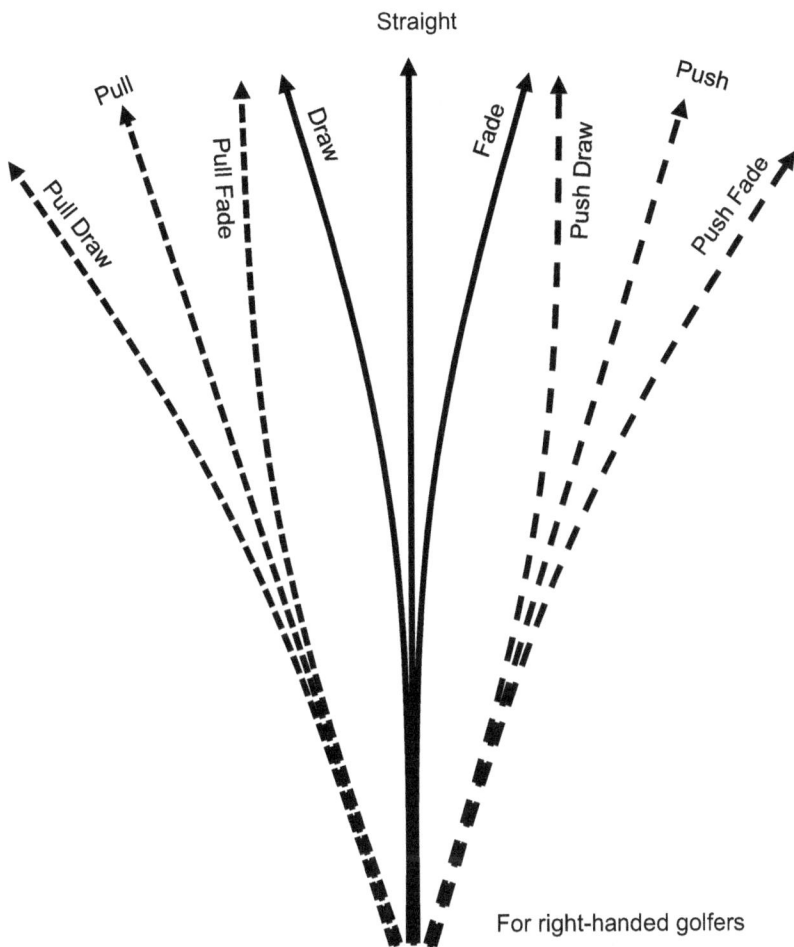

Fig. 1-3 Nine Ball Flight Patterns

In essence, there are only three basic ball flight patterns: straight, fade, and draw. The push, pull, and other combinations are just the three basic ball flight shapes launched in different directions, mostly by accident. In the following chapters, we will discuss what causes these ball flight patterns in golf.

2. Golf Ball and the Air

Have you ever wondered what it would be like to play golf on the moon? Well, an American astronaut can share his experience. On February 6, 1971, Alan Shepard, commander of Apollo 14, hit two golf balls on the moon with a makeshift 6-iron. Because of his cumbersome space suit, Alan could only swing the club with one hand. He shanked the first ball but managed to get the second one flying. According to Alan, the second ball traveled for "miles and miles and miles." That was quite impressive for a one-arm half swing. Today, his "Moon Club" is on display in the USGA Museum in Far Hills, New Jersey.

The gravity on the moon is only 1/6 that of the earth. That means a typical golf ball (1.62 ounces or 46g on the earth) weighs only 0.27 ounce or 7.7g on the moon. Obviously, the weaker gravity allows a ball to stay in the air longer and thus travel farther. Yet this is not the only reason.

According to NASA, the moon has a very thin atmosphere, which has so little gases that it would be considered a vacuum on the earth. The negligible air resistance also allows a ball to go faster and farther. Another interesting thing is that a golf shot on the moon would barely hook or slice no matter how it is struck.

On the moon, every golfer could potentially hit mile-long straight drives. Yet that might not be a good thing. If everyone could hit shots that are far and straight, then there wouldn't be much fun or excitement playing golf. The lack of challenge might just destroy this great game. Perhaps we should feel privileged to have the opportunity to play golf here on the earth. As we will discuss in the next section, the air is a crucial ingredient in the recipe that makes golf exhilarating, challenging, frustrating, and addictive.

WHAT IS SO SPECIAL ABOUT GOLF?

Among all the ball games, golf has earned the reputation as the most difficult to master. Every golfer, except Moe Norman, would agree it is indeed a tough job to have full control of the little ball.

What makes golf such a challenging sport? There are many contributing factors. For instance, the face of a club is much smaller in proportion to the ball when compared to tennis, Ping-Pong, or badminton. In addition, golf players must deal with clubs of different lengths and lofts, and it takes a confident mind and excellent body coordination to consistently hit solid shots, which are critical in a game that rewards precision.

However, one element really makes golf stand out: the ball spin. It is true that other ball games also involve spin; yet a ball travels a much longer distance in golf and the effects of spin will be amplified during the long ball flight and add tremendous unpredictability. When spin, speed, and distance are put together, things can quickly get very complicated. Among all these factors, ball spin plays the most important role, from the tee box to the green.

So what exactly is spin?

When an object moves around an axis, the movement is called rotation. If an object rotates around its own axis, this specific type of rotation is called spin. For example, the earth spins around an axis that goes from the North Pole to the South Pole while it circles around the Sun.

Most ball games involve spin and skillful players know how to take advantage of it in competitions. In tennis, players use topspin to keep the ball flying low; in Ping-Pong, players put spin on a ball to make it hard to receive; in soccer, banana kicks are all about imparting sidespin.

In golf, every ball spins while in motion. The flight distance and high ball speed amplify and dramatize the effects of spin. It is fair to say that golf would be a very boring game if spin weren't part of it. The bottom line is that spin is the foundation of golf. To understand golf ball flight, we must first understand the influence of ball spin.

Spin

In ball games, spin is named according to the direction of rotation. Let's look at the scenario where a ball spins around an axis that is parallel to the ground but perpendicular to the direction of travel. If the top of the ball rotates in the direction of travel (Fig. 2-1), we say the ball has topspin. When a golf ball rolls on the green, it has topspin.

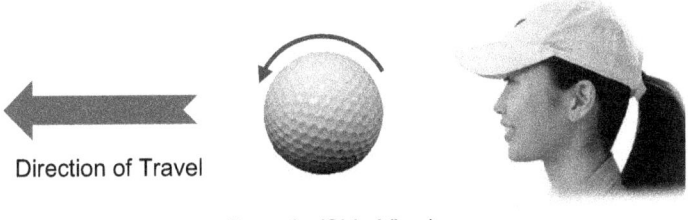

Topspin (Side View)

Fig. 2-1 Topspin

If the top of the ball rotates away from the direction of travel (Fig. 2-2), we say the ball has backspin. A golf ball flying in the air almost always has backspin and that is why we hear the word backspin on the Golf Channel all the time.

Backspin (Side View)

Fig. 2-2 Backspin

A ball's spin axis can point to any direction. If a ball spins around a vertical axis, which is the case when a basketball spins on a fingertip, we say the ball has sidespin. Based on the direction of its rotation from the bird's eye view, a ball can have either clockwise or counterclockwise sidespin.

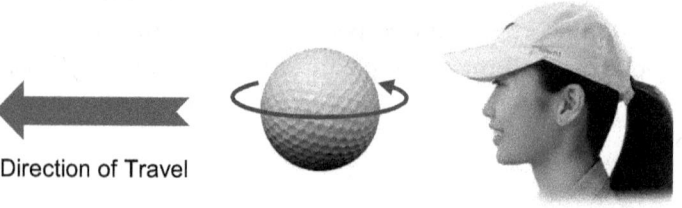

Counterclockwise Sidespin

Fig. 2-3 Sidespin

The backspin is an intrinsic element in the game of golf thanks to the design of golf clubs. When a golf ball is struck solidly by a lofted club, it is destined to launch with backspin. We will explain why this is the case in the following chapters. Even though ideally a golf ball can fly with pure backspin, in which the sidespin component is zero, in real world a golf ball launched into the air almost always exhibits a mixture of backspin and sidespin.

The spin by itself wouldn't affect a ball's trajectory, but an interesting phenomenon happens when a spinning golf ball travels through the air.

THE MAGNUS EFFECT

In the old days, golf balls were made with a smooth surface. Golfers back then noticed something strange: a beaten-up golf ball, whose cover was full of scratches, would travel much farther than a brand new one. That was quite counterintuitive since people assumed a rough surface meant stronger friction and therefore greater air resistance, which would result in a reduced carry distance. Apparently, that wasn't the case.

Later, scientists discovered that when a golf ball travels in the air with backspin, the rough surface actually helps create a lifting force, which allows the ball to stay airborne longer and travel farther.

This phenomenon was first investigated by German physicist Gustav Magnus and is known as the *Magnus Effect*.

Here is what happens: when a ball with a rough surface travels in the air, a lot of tiny turbulences are created along the border. For a ball with backspin, its top surface moves along with the air flow, and the turbulences cause the air to move along the top surface longer before separation. On the bottom, the rough surface moves against the air and generates stronger turbulences, which cause the air to separate from the ball sooner. Together, the actions on top and bottom produce a pressure difference, resulting in a force pointing upward.

For the same reason, a golf ball with topspin will experience a downward pull while flying in the air, and that is not a good thing in golf because it kills carry distance.

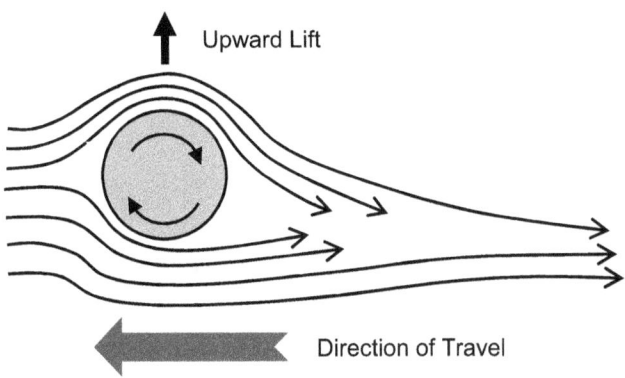

Fig. 2-4 Magnus Effect

Things are more complicated for a ball with a smooth surface. In this case, backspin doesn't typically produce an upward lift. This is why a golf ball full of scratches rises higher and travels farther than one with a smooth surface.

Obviously, collecting scratches on a golf ball would be a lengthy process, and the quality and consistency couldn't be guaranteed. Starting from 1905, golf balls have been manufactured with dimples to achieve better and more predictable aerodynamic performance.

In the game of golf, backspin is a desirable feature since golfers usually want their balls to stay airborne longer and travel farther. Backspin also helps a ball stop more quickly on the green. All golf clubs except putters are designed to produce backspin.

DIRECTION OF THE MAGNUS FORCE

Because of the Magnus Effect, a spinning ball with a rough surface will experience a Magnus force while traveling in the air. This force is perpendicular to the spin axis, as well as the direction of travel. Here is a little tip: the moving direction of a ball's front is the direction of the Magnus force.

For a ball with backspin, the resultant Magnus force points up to the sky. For a ball with topspin, the front of the ball moves downward, and the Magnus force points down to the ground, as shown in Fig. 2-5.

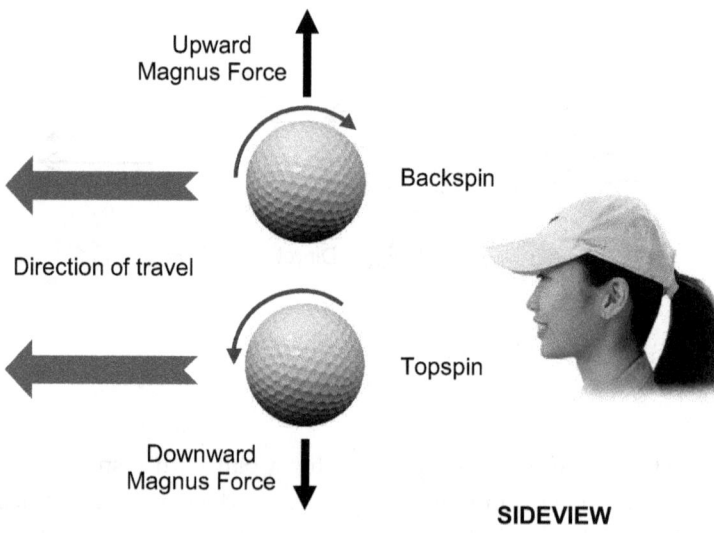

Fig. 2-5 Direction of the Magnus Force

From the bird's eye view, clockwise sidespin induces a right-pointing Magnus force. For right-handed golfers, this is the spin that results in a fade or slice. Counterclockwise sidespin, on the other hand, induces a Magnus force pointing left and is the draw or hook spin for right-handed golfers (Fig. 2-6).

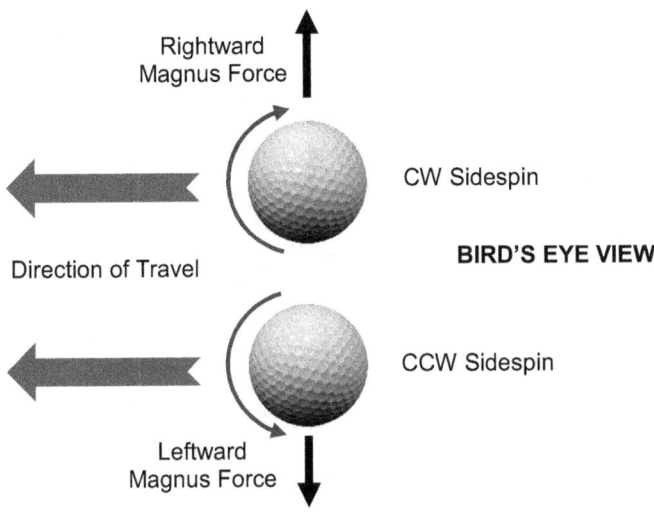

Fig. 2-6 Direction of the Magnus Force in Sidespin

DRAG REDUCTION

When a spinning ball travels in the air, the turbulence around it can reduce air resistance, which is also known as the drag. Reduced drag allows a golf ball to travel even farther.

For a ball to benefit from reduced air resistance, it must travel above a certain speed. Fortunately, the threshold speed is so low for balls with dimples that even a pitch shot can meet the requirement. The story is quite different for smooth balls. Without dimples, the speed threshold for drag reduction is so high that even a PGA tour player won't be able to reach it.

TILTED SPIN AXIS

For a ball in pure backspin, its spin axis is parallel to the ground and perpendicular to the direction of travel. The ball's spin equator stays in a vertical plane (Fig. 2-7).

Spin is a vector and it is represented by an arrow along the spin axis. The direction of the arrow follows the right-hand rule.

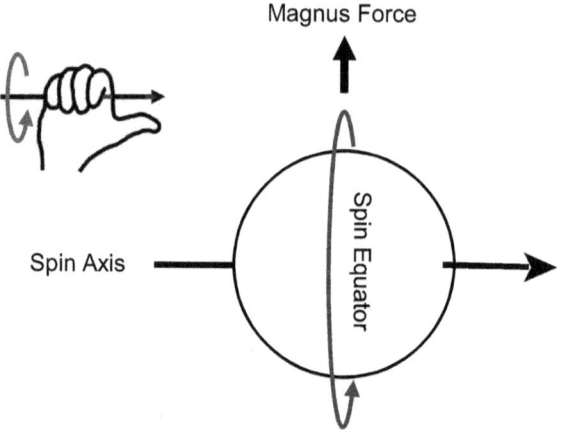

Fig. 2-7 Pure Backspin

In real world, a golf ball rarely flies with pure backspin; it is often launched into the air with a mixture of backspin and sidespin, as evidenced by data captured by launch monitors.

With the presence of sidespin, a ball's spin axis will no longer be parallel to the ground and will tilt to one side. The ball's spin equator will now be on a tilted plane. If gravity didn't exist, a ball would maintain the initial spin axis angle and continue traveling on this tilted plane. Yet the ubiquitous gravity on Earth makes this impossible, and a ball will soon fall off this tilted plane and curve left or right.

The following diagrams (Fig. 2-8 and Fig. 2-9) show what tilted spins look like and how they affect a ball's trajectory.

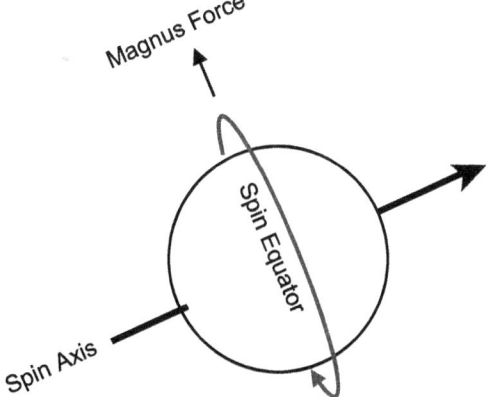

Spin tilting left causes the ball to curve left.

Fig. 2-8 Spin Tilting Left

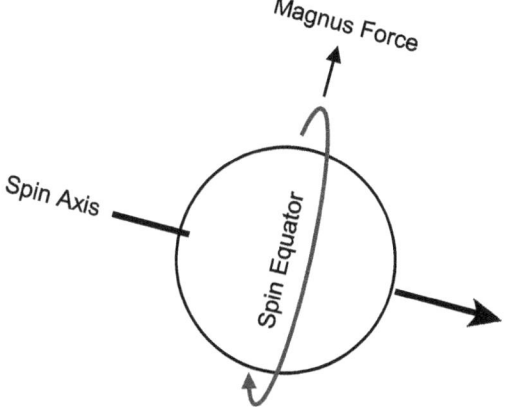

Spin tilting right causes the ball to curve right.

Fig. 2-9 Spin Tilting Right

Summary

- When a spinning ball with a rough surface travels in the air, it will experience a lateral Magnus force, which is perpendicular to the ball's travel direction and spin axis.
- The backspin is an intrinsic element in golf. A golf ball struck solidly by a lofted club will always launch with backspin.
- A golf ball with pure backspin tends to travel straight without curving left or right, and its spin axis is parallel to the ground.
- Backspin results in an upward lift, which fights gravity and keeps the ball airborne longer.
- Sidespin is a secondary element in golf. It induces a sideways force that causes a ball to curve left or right, depending on the direction of the sidespin.
- In a real-world scenario, a golf ball's spin axis is rarely perfectly parallel to the ground and is usually tilted at an angle.
- A tilted spin axis indicates that the spin contains both backspin and sidespin components.

3. Divide and Conquer

In physics and math, there is a very simple but extremely useful technique for analyzing and solving problems. It allows people to break down complex problems and solve them more effectively. This wonderful technique has a nerdy name: *vector decomposition*. It might sound sophisticated and intimidating, but that is really not the case. In fact, vector decomposition is easy to understand and simple to apply as long as you know how to draw some rectangles.

It is my belief that a golf book should not bring more stress to the game, thus physics jargons and math equations will be avoided as much as possible in this book. However, I do consider vector decomposition an exception. Having personally benefited so much from this tool, I am convinced that a basic understanding of vector decomposition would be valuable to golfers, especially those who have an inquisitive and analytical mind.

Vector and Scalar

In science, a quantity is either a vector or a scalar. A scalar is a quantity that only concerns magnitude, whereas a vector is a quantity that describes both magnitude and direction.

For example, *speed* is a scalar, and it only describes how fast an object moves. When talking about the speed of a car, we only care about how fast it can go. The direction of travel is irrelevant to the performance. A car traveling north at 100 mph and one going south at 100 mph both have the same speed and are equally fast. *Velocity*, on the other hand, is a vector and describes both how fast and in what direction an object moves. The two cars discussed earlier have different velocities. If the velocity of the car traveling north at 100 mph is V, then the velocity of the one going south at 100 mph is -V (negative V). In this book, the term "velocity" is used where it is academically necessary. Readers may feel free to replace it with "speed" if that makes things easier to understand.

A vector is commonly represented by an arrow in a graph. The length represents the magnitude and the arrowhead describes the direction (Fig. 3-1). The magnitude of a vector is proportional to the length of the line based on a predetermined scale.

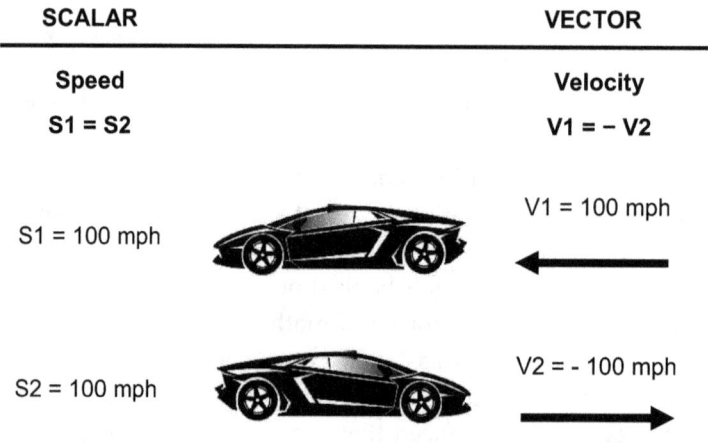

Fig. 3-1 Vector and Scalar

VECTOR COMPOSITION

Vectors make it easier to describe and analyze problems graphically in physics. In the process of solving problems, we often need to add two or more vectors together. The process of combining vectors is called *vector composition*, and it can be done easily using geometry. We will demonstrate how vector composition works in the following example.

A ball falls from the top of a building into a wind blowing horizontally. Assuming the wind force exerted on the ball is identical to the gravity in magnitude, in which direction does the ball fall?

To find the answer, we need to figure out the total force exerted on the ball. First, we draw two arrows (AB and AC) to represent the two force vectors, which in this case are the gravity and the wind force respectively (Fig. 3-2). The length of each arrow should be proportional to the magnitude of the force it represents, so these two arrows are identical in length. Next, we draw a rectangle using these two arrows as its two adjacent sides. The diagonal line (AD) of the rectangle represents the composition (or combination) of the gravity and the wind force. Pretty simple, isn't it? The total force is 2.29 oz., which can be calculated or measured from the graph.

It is obvious that the total force exerted on the ball points down at a 45° angle, and that is the direction along which the ball falls according to Newton's Law.

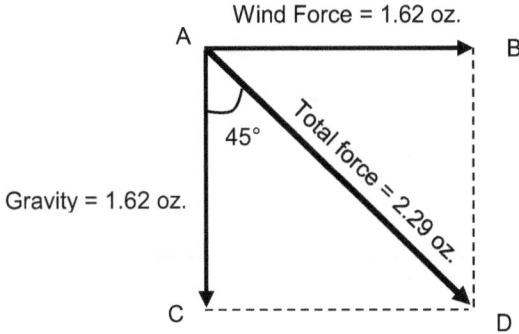

Fig. 3-2 Vector Composition

VECTOR DECOMPOSITION

A vector can also be broken down into two (or more) components so each can be analyzed separately. This process, which is called vector decomposition, makes it much easier for people to understand and solve a complex problem through the "divide and conquer" strategy.

It is a very useful technique in science. As we will demonstrate later, it is also an extremely valuable tool in the study of golf ball flight.

Decomposing a vector into two components is typically what we need in golf ball flight analyses, and it can be easily accomplished using the rectangle method. To do this, we first draw an arrow (AB) to represent the vector to be decomposed; then draw a rectangle using AB as its diagonal line (Fig. 3-3). Since different rectangles can be drawn based on the same diagonal line, we will have to determine the directions of the two adjacent sides (i.e., the directions for the two components) based on our interest or intention. Once the rectangle is drawn, its two adjacent sides (AC and AD) represent the two components of the original vector.

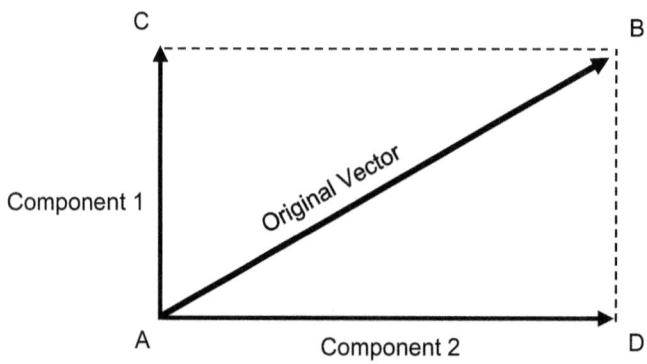

Fig. 3-3 Vector Decomposition using a Rectangle

Now let's take a look at how vector decomposition works in the following example.

A ballpark is 120 yards long and 90 yards wide. The diagonal line is therefore 150 yards, as shown in Fig. 3-4. Jack walks from corner A to corner B along the straight diagonal line while his friends, Sam and Wendy, watch from the sides.

It takes Jack one minute to walk from corner A to corner B and his velocity is therefore 150 yards per minute (ypm). First, we need to draw an arrow to represent V, Jack's velocity and we can simply use line AB in this case. In theory, we can draw an arrow of any length along the diagonal direction to represent V, the rectangle will change proportionally and the result will be the same. Next, we draw a rectangle to decompose Jack's velocity. Since we are interested in the north and the east directions, two adjacent sides of the decomposition rectangle should be drawn along north and east respectively. In this case, the decomposition rectangle (ABCD) happens to be the same as the one representing the ballpark, although it could be proportionally bigger or smaller.

Now we have the two components of Jack's velocity (V). The component in the north direction, V1, is represented by AC; and the component in the east direction, V2, is represented by AD. Each component's magnitude is proportional to the length of the line representing it and its direction is indicated by the arrow head.

Either by calculation or direct measurement, we can figure out the magnitude of V1 and V2, which are 90 and 120 ypm respectively. This makes perfect sense because from Wendy's perspective Jack moves 90 yards north in one minute. Similarly, Sam sees Jack walk 120 yards east during the same time period.

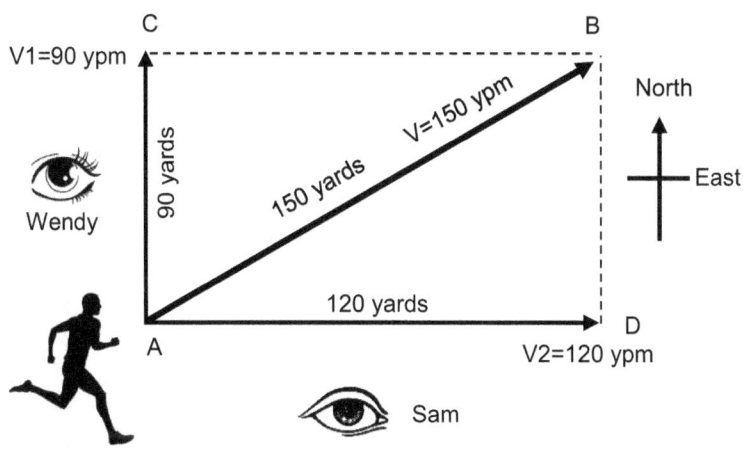

Fig. 3-4 Vector Decomposition

We just explained the concept of vector decomposition and demonstrated how a velocity vector could be decomposed into two components using the rectangle method. Let's review the steps:
1. Draw an arrow to represent the original vector.
2. Choose two directions of interest, which are perpendicular to each other in our analyses.
3. Draw a rectangle using the original vector as a diagonal line. The two adjacent sides of the rectangle should match the directions of interest.
4. The two adjacent sides then represent the two components of the original vector.

Now let's look at another example. An archer shoots an arrow along a 45° launch angle at a speed of 100 mph (Fig. 3-5). We want to figure out how far the arrow travels before it hits the ground. This problem could have been a tough nut to crack, but with vector decomposition it can be solved easily.

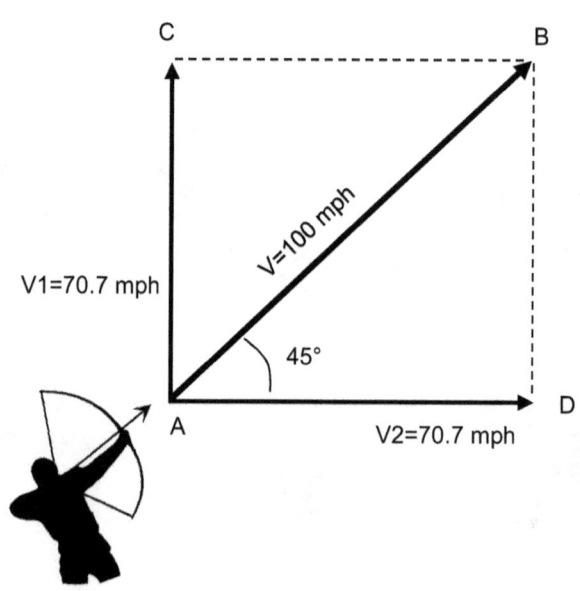

Fig. 3-5 Arrow Velocity Decomposition

We will choose to decompose the arrow's velocity along the vertical and horizontal directions. The velocity's vertical component fights gravity and determines how long the arrow can stay in the air, whereas the horizontal component determines how far the arrow travels before it hits the ground.

First, we draw a diagonal line (AB) at 45° to represent the arrow's velocity V. We then draw a rectangle around the diagonal line, with vertical and horizontal sides. In this particular case, the rectangle happens to be a square. The two adjacent sides of the square, AC and AD, represent the two components of the arrow's velocity in those directions.

V1 is the vertical component and represented by AC. It points up to the sky and is 70.7 mph in magnitude according to the calculation. V2 is the horizontal component, which points to the target. V2's magnitude is also 70.7 mph. Knowing V1, we can figure out how long the arrow stays in the air. We can then find out how far the arrow will travel within its airborne time. We will skip the details of the calculation since they are not important to our discussions here.

As a side note, vector decomposition in general can be done using a parallelogram and the two components can point in any directions. For golf ball flight analyses however, a rectangle, which is a special kind of parallelogram, is sufficient because the two components we are interested in happen to be perpendicular to each other.

4. Spin and Impact

Since spin plays a critical role in the game of golf, understanding how it is produced is crucial to the study of ball flight. In golf, spin results from the "moment of truth," i.e., the collision between a lofted clubface and a ball. In this extremely brief process, the clubhead transfers part of its kinetic energy to the ball. Some of the transferred energy drives the ball into the air and some makes the ball spin. Now, we will study how the energy distribution at impact affects ball speed, spin rate, spin axis, and launch angle.

Perpendicular Collision

For simplicity, we will use a metal block to model the iron clubhead when analyzing the clubhead-ball collision (Fig. 4-1). The three-dimensional (3D) block will be represented by a rectangle in the two-dimensional (2D) diagrams.

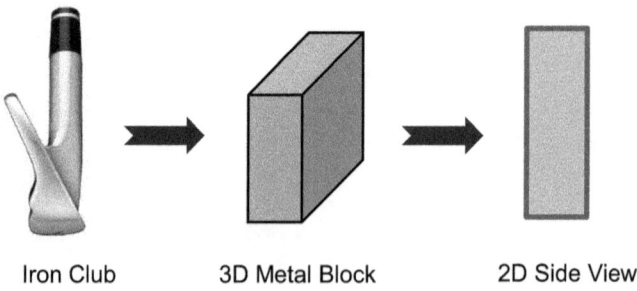

Iron Club   3D Metal Block   2D Side View

Fig. 4-1 A Simplified Clubhead Model

Let's first define some commonly used terms. *Face normal* is used to describe the orientation of a clubface and is represented by a dash-line arrow that is perpendicular to the clubface and also passes through the club's CG (Center of Gravity). *Face parallel* refers to the direction parallel to the clubface.

Although CM (Center of Mass) is the proper term here, CG will be used in this book because of its popularity among golfers. In non-academic settings, CM and CG are often used interchangeably.

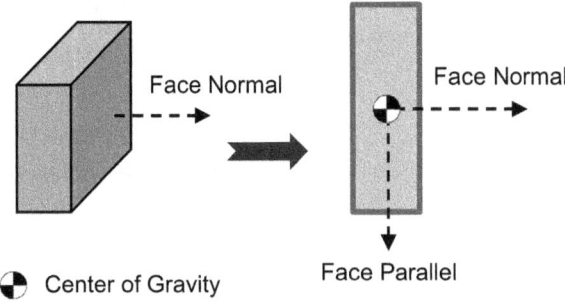

Fig. 4-2 Face Normal

Clubhead velocity defines both the speed and moving direction of a clubhead and is represented by a solid arrow originating from the club's CG. The length of the arrow represents the magnitude (speed) and the arrowhead indicates the club's moving direction (Fig. 4-3).

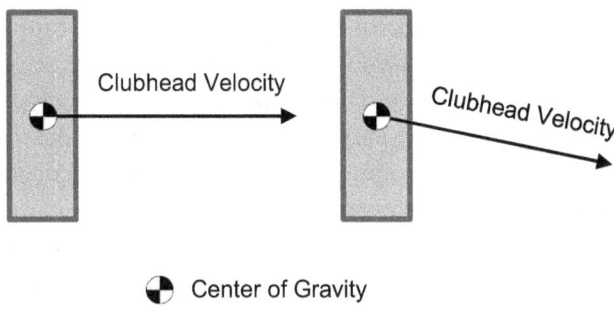

Fig. 4-3 Clubhead Velocity

As we will soon find out, the *angular relation between the face normal and clubhead velocity* is the most important parameter in golf ball flight study.

Unless stated otherwise, we normally assume the clubhead's CG, the impact point, and the ball's CG are on a straight line (the face normal) when analyzing the clubhead-ball collision, as shown in Fig. 4-4. This is the requirement for solid ball striking.

If the clubhead velocity and the face normal point in the same direction at impact, we call such an impact a *perpendicular collision* (Fig. 4-4). Keep in mind, *an object's moving direction is the direction of its velocity at any given moment.*

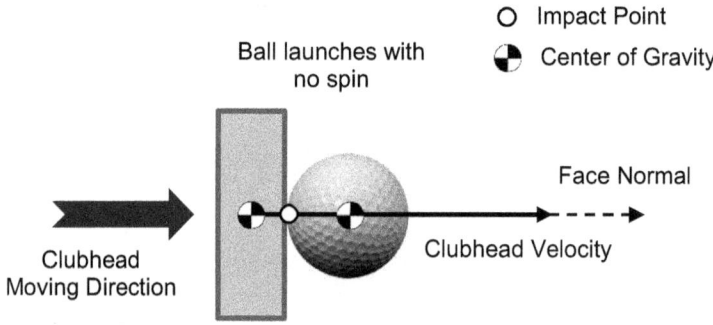

Fig. 4-4 A Perpendicular Collision

In a perpendicular collision, the entirety of the clubhead velocity is distributed in the face normal direction. The ball won't spin after impact because the impact force points through the ball's CG and produces no torque. As we know, torque is required to make an object spin or rotate. The clubhead won't twist either because the reaction force exerted back on it by the ball also passes through its CG and produces zero torque. In a solid perpendicular collision, the resultant ball speed is maximized.

When dropping a golf ball onto a leveled hard surface, we create a perpendicular collision, and the ball will bounce up with no spin. Although a perfect perpendicular collision barely happens in the game of golf, it is an important aspect in ball flight analyses.

OBLIQUE COLLISION

What happens when a clubhead approaches a ball with its face oblique to its moving direction? Now, the velocity vector and the face normal point in different directions (Fig. 4-5). We will call this an *oblique collision*. Again, we assume the two CGs and the impact point are on a straight line.

During an oblique collision, the clubhead exerts a force on the ball via the impact point. In this case, the total force no longer points through the ball's CG and thus produces a torque, which causes the ball to spin.

The ball striking action using a lofted golf club is an oblique collision. With the clubhead velocity and face normal pointing in different directions, things gets a little complicated.

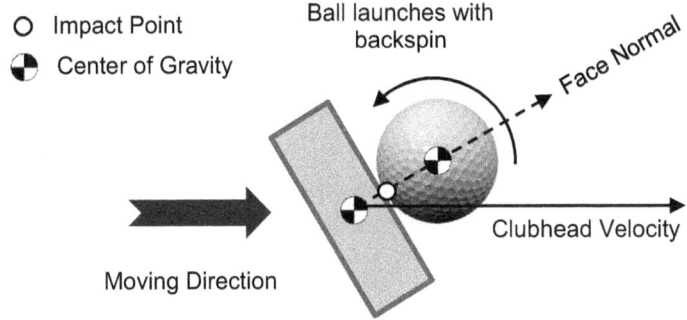

Fig. 4-5 An Oblique Collision

IMPACT ANALYSIS

To understand what transpires during an oblique collision, we are going to enlist the magical tool, vector decomposition, to analyze the interaction between the clubhead and the ball.

Here we assume the clubface tilts back at a 30° angle, and the clubhead velocity V is 100 mph pointing right (Fig. 4-6). The tilt angle is referred to as the loft in golf. The setup shown in Fig. 4-6 is similar to that of a 6-iron.

29

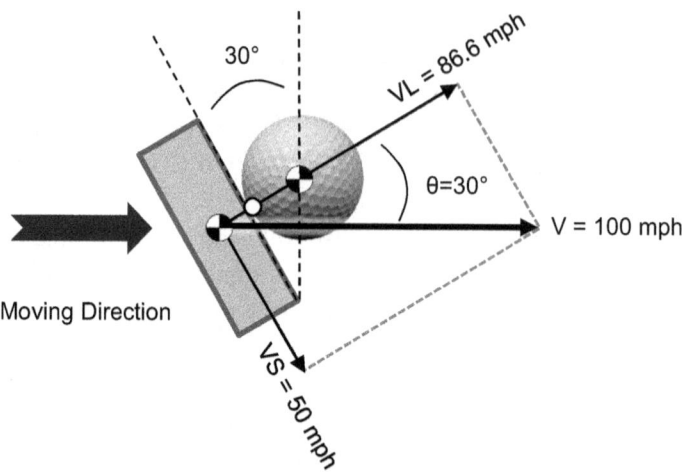

Fig. 4-6 Oblique Collision Analysis

The clubhead velocity V can be easily decomposed into two components using the rectangle method. The key decision here is choosing the directions for the two components. In this case, we are interested in what happens in the face normal and face parallel directions. The two adjacent sides of the decomposition rectangle are therefore determined.

As shown in Fig. 4-6, the clubhead velocity V is decomposed into VL and VS along the two directions chosen. In case you are wondering, L stands for launch and S for spin. Detailed explanations will be offered in a moment.

We can quickly evaluate each component's relative magnitude by the length of the arrows in Fig. 4-6. Obviously, VL is greater than VS in this particular case and such an evaluation is sufficient for most golfers. For those who are interested in knowing the exact magnitude of each component, the following equations can be used:

VL = V * cos (θ)
VS = V * sin (θ)

In Fig. 4-6, θ is 30° and V is 100 mph. Therefore we can calculate the magnitude of VL and VS:

VL = V * cos (30°) = 0.866V = 86.6 mph
VS = V * sin (30°) = 0.5V = 50 mph

LAUNCH VECTOR VL

Vector decomposition tells us that in the face normal direction the clubhead approaches the ball at velocity VL (Fig. 4-7). Looks familiar? This is the perpendicular collision we discussed earlier, except that the whole setup is now tilted at an angle. The influence of gravity at impact is trivial and will be ignored here. After the collision, part of the clubhead's kinetic energy is transferred to the ball, which quickly launches off at velocity VBN in the face normal direction.

Since the primary job of VL (the clubhead velocity's component in the face normal direction) is to launch a ball into the air, in this book we call it the *launch vector*.

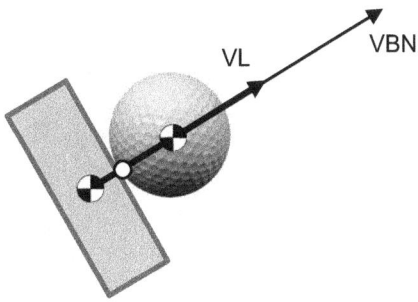

Fig. 4-7 Launch Vector VL

VBN, which is the primary contributor to a ball's total launch velocity, is mainly determined by launch vector VL, along with the weights of the clubhead and the ball. VL also determines the impact force, impact pressure, and consequently the friction between the ball and the clubface. Given the same clubhead speed, a club with a higher loft produces a weaker launch vector VL, as shown in Fig. 4-6, and usually results in a lower ball speed and a shorter carry distance.

SPINNING VECTOR VS

At impact, the clubhead moves downwards at velocity VS in the face parallel direction. For a driver or fairway wood with a curved face, face parallel would be the direction tangential to the impact point.

In the face parallel direction, the clubhead approaches and makes contact with the ball, and its movement (VS) causes the ball to move along through the work of friction. At impact, the ball exerts on the clubhead a tremendous amount of pressure, which quickly increases as the ball is compressed and then decreases as the ball bounces away. During the brief engagement, which lasts about half a millisecond, the ball initially slides up on the clubface as it tries to catch up speed, and then quickly starts rolling, creating backspin (Fig. 4-8). In this book, we will call the clubhead velocity's component in the face parallel direction, VS, the *spinning vector* because its primary function is to produce ball spin.

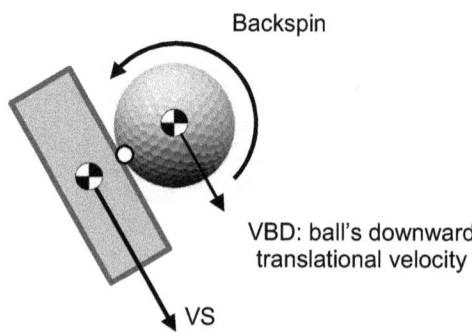

Fig. 4-8 Spinning Vector VS

VS also causes the ball to move down with a translational velocity VBD in the face parallel direction. Yes, even though the ball rolls up the clubface during impact, it actually moves downward with reference to the ground. If you find this confusing, think about a passenger running towards the back of a moving train. In the eyes of a spectator standing on the ground, the passenger still moves forward with the train.

In fact, this translational velocity VBD plays a noticeable role in golf ball flight. It not only contributes to a ball's launch speed, but also affects the launch angle. We will discuss this in more details later.

Spin Experiments

The following experiments demonstrate how a moving surface can impart both spin and translational velocity to a ball. To set up for the experiments, put a golf ball on a letter-size cardboard, which is placed near the edge of a table, as shown in Fig. 4-9.

Experiment One: pull the cardboard away at a moderate speed and we will see the ball rolls (spins) back on the surface. This is because the friction the cardboard exerts on the bottom of the ball creates a torque around the ball's CG and causes the ball to spin. When the ball rolls purely, its bottom and the cardboard have the same speed, whereas its top, as well as its CG, moves in the opposite direction on the cardboard.

In the end, the ball will be dragged away from its original location marked on the table by the cardboard (Fig. 4-9). This is an indication that the rolling ball has also acquired a translational velocity and its CG moves in the same direction as the cardboard, only at a lower speed.

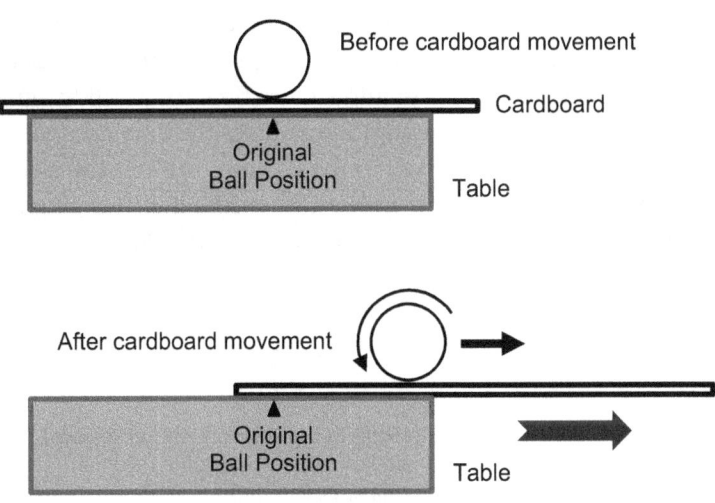

Fig. 4-9 Spin Experiments

Experiment Two: set up again, this time pull the cardboard away as fast as you can. Notice the ball barely moves away from its original location marked on the table and it doesn't spin much either.

Since the friction stays the same, with a higher cardboard speed it takes longer for the ball to accelerate to the state of pure rolling, in which the ball's bottom would move along with the cardboard at the same speed. In the second experiment, pure rolling isn't achieved in time and the ball slides and rolls simultaneously when it leaves the cardboard. Both the spin rate and the translational speed fail to reach their maximum achievable values.

SPIN RATE AND BALL SPEED

What happens in the face parallel direction during golf ball striking resembles putting a ball onto a fast-moving conveyor belt. In both scenarios, a stationary ball makes contact with a moving surface. What happens in the experiments is slightly different as both the ball and cardboard are at rest initially. However, the general principles are the same and similar actions can be observed in golf.

Given enough time, a ball put on a moving conveyor belt will eventually stop sliding and reach pure rolling. How quickly it can start pure rolling is determined by the speed of the belt and the friction. A higher belt speed requires more time for a ball to achieve pure rolling, whereas stronger friction reduces the time needed.

When a ball starts rolling purely, its spin rate and translational speed reach their respective maximum values for the given belt speed. Both can be calculated using the equations in Fig. 4-10.

$$SR = 145 * V_{BELT}$$

$$V_{BALL} = V_{BELT} * 2 / 7$$

SR: Ball's Spin Rate in rpm (revolution per minute)
V_{BALL}: Ball's translational speed in mph
V_{BELT}: Conveyor belt speed in mph

Fig. 4-10 Speed and Spin Rate for a Ball in Pure Rolling

These equations reveal some interesting relationships. When pure rolling is achieved, the ball's translational speed and spin rate will reach their maximum values. For instance, if the belt speed is 100 mph, then a ball in pure rolling will have a speed of 28.6 mph and a spin rate of 14500 rpm.

According to the law of conservation of angular momentum, the ball speed and the spin rate maintain a fixed ratio, which is true whether the ball is in pure rolling or not. In other words, the higher a ball's translational speed (with reference to the ground), the faster it spins, and vice versa.

When a ball is both rolling and sliding, its actual translational speed and spin rate will be lower than the maximum values shown in the equations listed above.

These relationships are also valid in golf ball striking and the details will be discussed in the next chapter.

5. Straight Shots

In this chapter and the next one, we will discuss how different types of collision in golf produce various ball flight patterns. We will be looking at golf impact mainly from two viewpoints: the bird's eye view and the face-on view.

Keep it Square

The word "square" is ubiquitous in the golf world and is mainly used to describe clubface orientation or a golfer's body alignment. For example, an instructor may ask his student to "get the clubface square to the target line."

It is important that we clarify the meaning of "square" in golf. Literally, "square" in such a context means "perpendicular" or "at a right angle." Since we need a reference when talking about orientation or alignment, the target line has been the natural choice for most, although not all, scenarios.

What does an instructor mean when he asks a student to set the clubface square to the target line? Apparently, he is not talking about getting the actual clubface perpendicular to the target line since that would eliminate the loft and make no sense at all. What the instructor really wants his student to do is to keep the *grooves* on the clubface perpendicular to the target line (Fig. 5-1). Ideally, these grooves should also be parallel to the ground at impact in order to hit straight shots. Getting the face normal pointing towards the target would also set the clubface square to the target line, and this definition works better for woods, which might not have grooves on their sweet spots at all.

Y-PLANE

Imagine a plane that is perpendicular to the grooves and passes through the CG of the clubhead. We will call it the *Y-plane* because it runs in the vertical direction (Y axis) of the clubface. Y-plane makes clubface orientation discussions easier. A clubface is square to the target line as long as the Y-plane sits vertically on it, regardless of the loft change. The face normal is always inside the Y-plane.

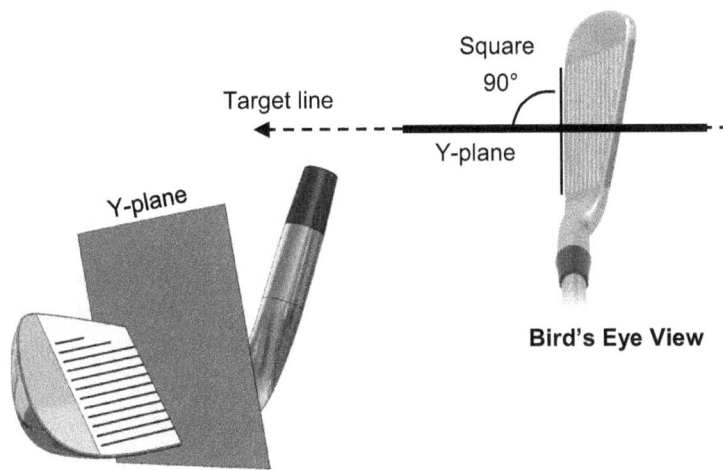

Fig. 5-1 Clubface Being Square to the Target Line

Besides the square setup, a clubface can also be open or closed to the target line, as shown in Fig. 5-2 and Fig. 5-3. In either scenario, the target line intersects the Y-plane.

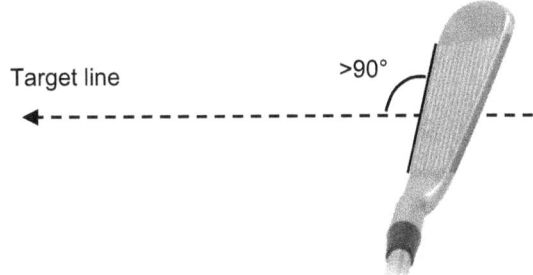

Fig. 5-2 Clubface Being Open to the Target Line

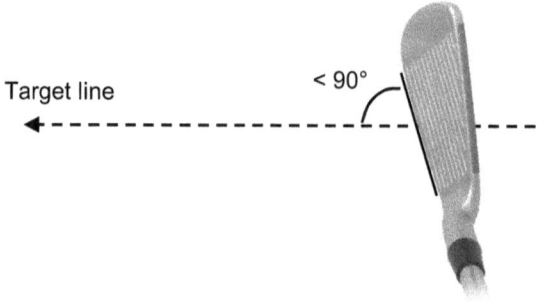

Fig. 5-3 Clubface Being Closed to the Target Line

Several conditions must be met to hit a straight target-seeking shot, the primary requirement is that the clubface must be square to the target line at impact. We will talk more about this in a moment.

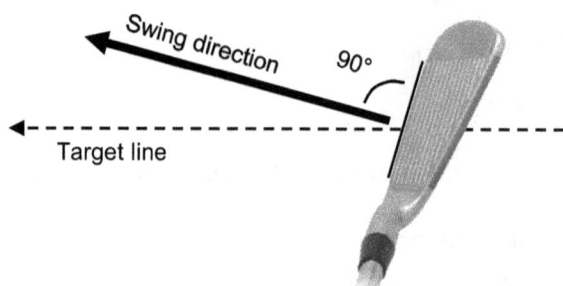

Fig. 5-4 Clubface Square to Swing Direction

SQUARE TO SWING DIRECTION

We can also use other references for clubface orientation, such as the clubhead's swing direction or clubhead velocity. In Fig. 5-4, the clubface is open to the target line, but square to the clubhead velocity or swing direction. Some people would describe this as "clubface square to the swing path." In this case, the Y-plane contains the club velocity vector. *In golf ball flight analyses, clubface alignment with reference to clubhead velocity or club swing direction is far more important and meaningful.*

To hit a straight shot, we must set up for a square strike: at impact, the clubface is square to the clubhead velocity and the grooves are parallel to the ground. That means the clubhead velocity vector is in a vertically erected Y-plane. To deliver this straight shot to the target, the target line must also be in the Y-plane.

Neutral Shaft Position

We say a club is in the neutral shaft position (or simply neutral position) when its grooves are parallel to the ground and its shaft appears to point straight up from the face-on view, as if the shaft was placed against a vertical wall (Fig. 5-5). The shaft neither leans towards nor tilts away from the target.

Club Loft

Club loft is the angle between the clubface and the shaft from the face-on view, as shown in Fig. 5-5. This number can be found on the specification sheet provided by the club manufacturer.

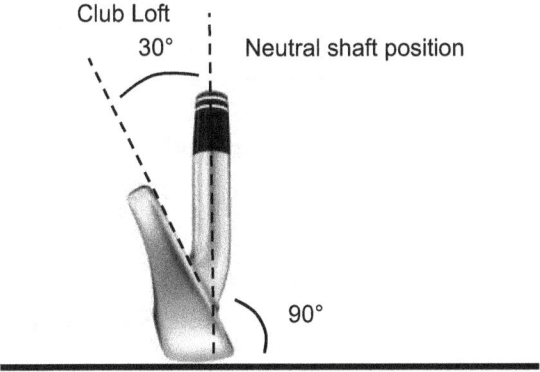

Fig. 5-5 Club Loft

EFFECTIVE LOFT

The angle between clubface normal and the ground at the moment of impact is called the *effective loft*, also known as the *dynamic loft* in many launch monitors (Fig. 5-6). When a club is in neutral shaft position, its effective loft is the same as the club loft.

I consider effective loft a more appropriate term for the actual loft presented at impact. Dynamic loft would be more suitable for describing the clubface inclination, which changes dynamically throughout a golf swing, at any given moment. Or we can say the effective loft is a club's dynamic loft at impact.

In golf, a ball's launch angle is primarily determined by the effective loft and is technically irrelevant to the club loft.

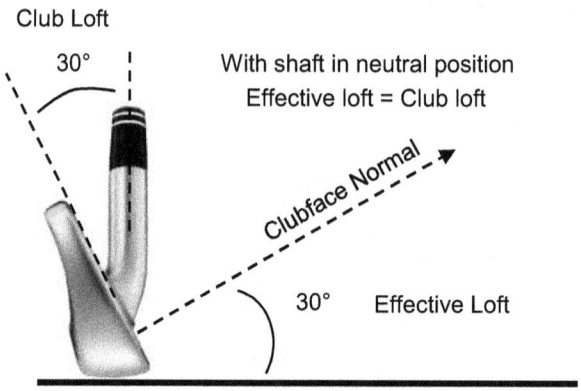

Fig. 5-6 Effective Loft

In actual ball striking, the effective loft doesn't typically have the same value as the club loft because the shaft is seldom in the neutral position at impact. For example, with its shaft leaning forward 10° at impact, a 30° 6-iron presents an effective loft of 20° (Fig. 5-7).

Things can be more complicated for a driver, which typically has a curved clubface. Its effective loft is also dependent on the impact location: a higher impact location presents a greater effective loft.

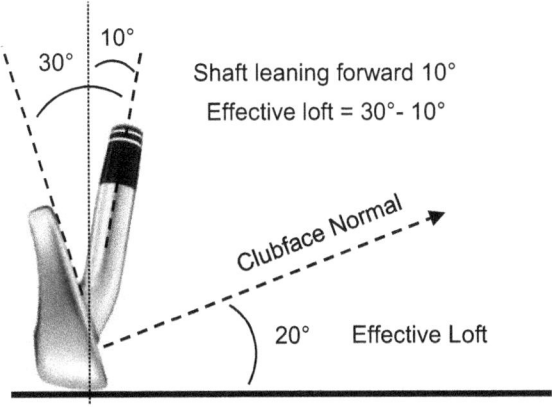

Fig. 5-7 Effective Loft

Spin Loft

Per our discussion in Chapter Four, the angle between clubhead velocity and clubface normal is critical to the magnitude of the spinning vector, and is therefore given the name *spin loft* (Fig. 5-8).

For a specific clubhead speed, a higher spin loft results in a stronger spinning vector VS, which typically produces a higher spin rate. The spin loft is zero in a perpendicular collision, so is the spin.

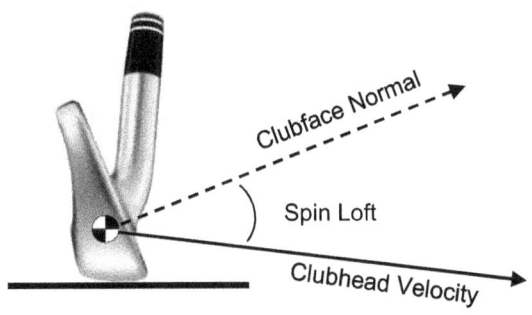

Fig. 5-8 Spin Loft

ANGLE OF ATTACK

In actual golf shots, the clubhead velocity or swing direction at impact isn't necessarily parallel to the ground. For instance, the clubhead in a solid iron shot typically travels downward at impact, hitting the ball first and the ground second. In contrast, the clubhead in a drive usually moves upward to strike a ball.

The angle between the clubhead velocity and the ground at the moment of impact is called *angle of attack* or *attack angle* (Fig. 5-9). In popular launch monitors, the attack angle in a downward strike is given a negative number, whereas that in an upward strike is defined as positive.

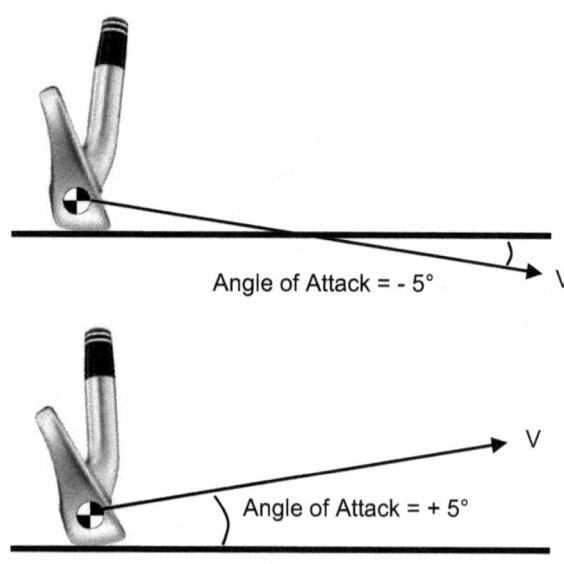

Fig. 5-9 Angle of Attack

How They Are Related

Neither the club loft nor the effective loft has direct influence on the spin loft or spinning vector. Nonetheless, spin loft and effective loft are indirectly related through angle of attack, as shown in the following equation.

Spin Loft = Effective Loft – Attack Angle

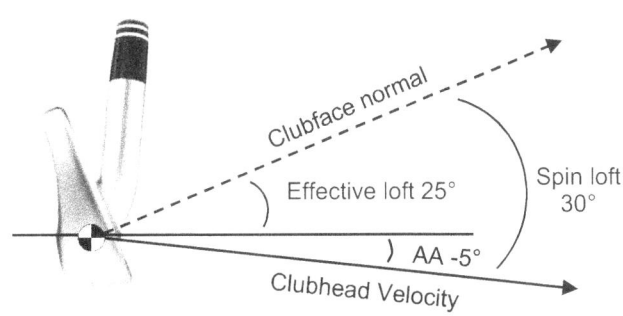

Spin Loft = Effective Loft – Attack Angle
In this case, Spin loft = 25° - (-5°) = 30°

Fig. 5-10 Spin Loft, Effective Loft, and Attack Angle

Do we produce a higher spin rate by hitting down on a ball? Not necessarily. By keeping the same clubhead speed and effective loft, hitting down will increase spin loft and therefore boost spin rates. However, if we reduce the effective loft by 5° in order to hit down with a -5° attack angle, then the spin loft doesn't change, nor does the spin rate, assuming the clubhead speed stays the same.

Clubhead Velocity at Impact

We will now study the square strike scenario, where the clubface at impact is square to the swing direction (not the target line). In this case, the clubhead velocity vector is contained in the Y-plane. By substituting the metal block in Fig. 4-6 with an iron club, we arrive at Fig. 5-11. Per discussions in the previous chapter, the clubhead velocity can be decomposed into components along the face normal and face parallel directions.

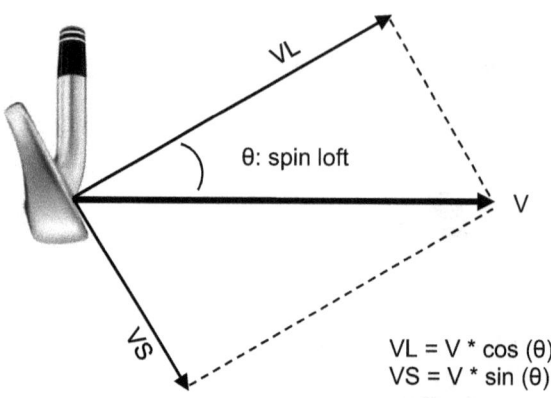

Fig. 5-11 Clubhead Velocity Decomposition

To decompose the clubhead velocity along the face normal and face parallel directions, we need to know the clubhead speed and the spin loft. *Neither the club loft nor the effective loft matters here.* The decomposition of V produces launch vector VL and spinning vector VS.

The magnitude of each component can be calculated using the equations in Fig. 5-11 or directly measured from the diagram. For a spin loft of 30°, VL is 0.866V and VS is 0.5V in magnitude.

Launch Vector VL

In the face normal direction, the clubhead approaches the ball at velocity VL and strikes it into the air. Assuming solid contact is made at impact, the ball will launch with an initial velocity of VBN (B stands for ball and N for normal) in the face normal direction. Please keep in mind that VBN is only one component of the total ball velocity, and is the more important one.

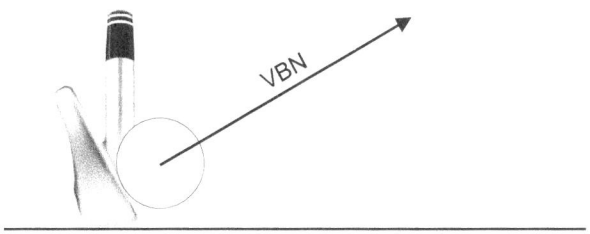

Fig. 5-12 VBN

A precise VBN calculation can be complicated, but we can get a close estimation. Equation [1] in Fig. 5-13 calculates the magnitude of VBN in a perfect elastic collision, where there is no loss of kinetic energy. However, real-world ball striking is not an elastic collision since some kinetic energy will be lost. Equation [2] shows the calculation of VBN in an inelastic collision, which is more realistic. It factors in the loss of kinetic energy by using the Coefficient of Restitution (e), which is limited to 0.83 by the USGA.

$$VBN = 2M_C * VL / (M_C + M_B) \quad [1]$$

$$\mathbf{VBN = (1 + e) * M_C * VL / (M_C + M_B)} \quad [2]$$

Where:
M_C: weight of the clubhead (250 ~ 300 grams)
M_B: weight of the ball (45 grams)
e: Coefficient of Restitution (approximately 0.83)

Fig. 5-13 VBN Estimation

For example, if the clubhead weighs 270g and the ball weighs 45g in Fig. 5-11, the VBN produced by a clubhead speed of 85mph and a spin loft of 30° can be calculated as follows.

VBN = (1+0.83) * 270 * (85 * cos (30°))/ (270+45)
    = 1.83 * 270 * (85 * 0.866)/ (270+45)
    = 115.5 (mph)

Spinning Vector VS

In the face parallel direction, the clubhead travels down at velocity VS, and the surface friction causes the ball to move down along at velocity VBD (B stands for ball and D for downward). In the meantime, the ball rolls up the clubface, producing backspin.

VBD is the other component of the total ball velocity. The composition of the two components, VBN and VBD, produces the total ball velocity VB, as shown in Fig. 5-14. VBD not only contributes to a ball's total speed but also causes its launch trajectory to shift from the face normal towards the ground.

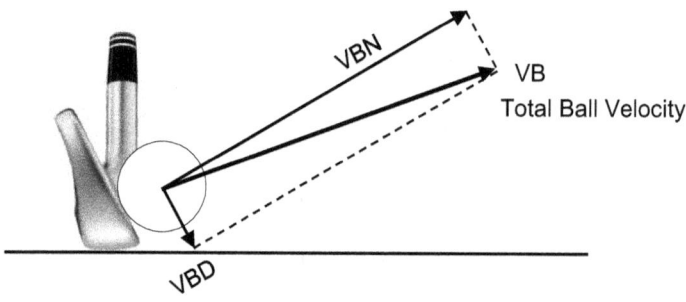

Fig. 5-14 Total Ball Velocity VB

THE IMPORTANT EQUATIONS FOR BALL FLIGHT

Now let's review what we learned in Chapter Four. Given enough time, a ball on the conveyor belt will eventually reach pure rolling with predictable speed and spin rate, both of which are determined by the speed of the belt, as shown in Fig. 4-10. Once in the pure rolling state, the ball speed and spin rate reach their respective maximum values for the given belt speed and will no longer increase.

In a golf shot, a ball's initial movement on the face also starts with sliding, just like a ball placed on a moving belt. The difference is: in golf a ball makes contact with the clubface only briefly and doesn't always have enough time to reach pure rolling, depending on the friction and the magnitude of VS.

Straight Shots

A ball can reach pure rolling before leaving the clubface if the ball-clubface friction is strong enough, then it will achieve the maximum spin rate and VBD corresponding to the spinning vector in that particular shot, as shown in Fig. 5-15. Staying on the clubface after pure rolling won't further increase the spin rate.

Conversely, a ball's spin rate will be lower than the maximum value if it launches off the clubface while still sliding. This can happen when the ball-clubface friction falls short of the threshold needed to reach pure rolling in time, as in some wedge shots. Spin reduction may also happen when a ball deforms too much in a high speed drive that it no longer rolls effectively.

For a solid shot where pure rolling is achieved, we will be able to calculate critical ball flight data by using the two equations listed in Fig. 5-15. If math or physics gives you a headache, feel free to skip them and jump to the explanations followed.

$$SR = 145 * VS$$
$$VBD = VS * 2 / 7$$

SR: Spin rate in rpm (revolution per minute)
VBD: Ball speed in mph in face parallel direction
VS: Spinning vector's magnitude in mph, VS = V * sin(Spin_Loft)
V: Clubhead speed in mph

Fig. 5-15 Important Ball Flight Data

Based on the law of conservation of angular momentum, *the spin rate is always proportional to VBD, whether the ball is in pure rolling or not*. Their relationship can be described by the following equation, where spin rate SR is in rpm and VBD is in mph.

SR = 505 * VBD

According to this equation, a spin rate of 5000 rpm corresponds to a VBD of 10 mph. This explains why a higher spin rate usually results in a lower launch angle.

We can learn a number of interesting things from the three equations mentioned above. Let me explain them in plain language.

1. For any given golf shot, there exist a maximum spin rate and a maximum VBD, both of which are determined by the magnitude of the spinning vector (VS).
2. Once a ball achieves pure rolling, both VBD and spin rate will reach their maximal values.
3. A higher spin rate means a higher VBD, which consequently results in a higher ball speed and a lower launch angle.
4. The ball-clubface friction is especially important for shots involve high-loft wedges, which typically produce a stronger spinning vector and thus require stronger friction to stop ball sliding in time. For instance, the spinning vector is about 20 mph for a 10-degree driver swung at 115 mph, but can be 66 mph for a 56-degree sand wedge swung at 80 mph.
5. For a given spin loft, a higher swing speed usually produces a higher spin rate. Tour pros can produce higher spin rates than amateurs partially because they swing faster.
6. VBD is usually much lower in magnitude than VBN, the ball velocity component in the face normal direction. Hence VB is mainly determined by VBN.

The friction between the ball and the clubface is affected by multiple factors, including ball construction, impact pressure, groove profile, and interfacial conditions, etc. Common spin killers in high-loft shots include hard ball cover materials, worn-out or dirty grooves, and juicy grass blades caught between the ball and the clubface, etc.

LAUNCH ANGLE

In golf, *launch angle*, or more appropriately the *vertical launch angle*, is defined as the angle between a ball's launch velocity VB (or its initial moving direction) and the ground, as shown in Fig. 5-16.

Due to the contribution of VBD, a ball's launch velocity (VB) deviates from face normal and will not be perpendicular to the clubface, as shown in Fig. 5-14. Therefore, a ball's launch angle is always smaller than the effective loft. In this book, we will call the difference between them the *vertical deviation angle*.

The vertical deviation angle is determined by the ratio of VBD to VBN. If VBN stays the same, increasing VBD will cause a ball to launch lower. Considering the relationship between spin rate and VBD, we know a higher spin rate usually results in a lower launch angle, especially for wedges. This pattern is well reflected in data collected by launch monitors.

VBD, as well as spin rate and vertical deviation angle, is determined by multiple factors, including spin loft, impact location, golf ball material, and the club used. As a rule of thumb, a club with a higher loft typically produces a greater vertical deviation angle.

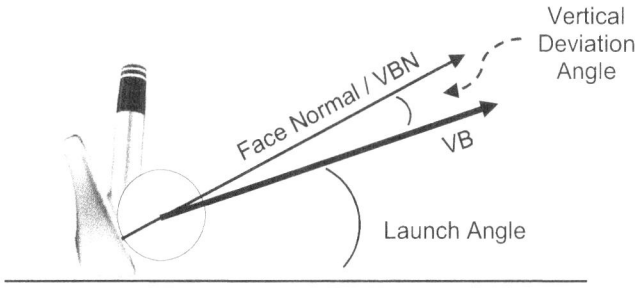

Fig. 5-16 The Launch Angle

Assuming pure rolling is achieved, the vertical deviation angle in an ideal shot can be calculated using the equations in Fig. 5-13 and 5-15. According to the derived equation, the vertical deviation angle is not affected by the clubhead speed when a ball has achieved pure rolling; it is determined by the following factors:
- Spin loft
- Clubhead weight
- Ball weight

The vertical deviation angle is about 18~23% of the spin loft, depending on the club used. It is approximately 18% for drivers and fairway woods; and 23% for wedges. For a rough estimation of the vertical deviation angle, we can use 20% of the spin loft across the board (Fig. 5-17). When the spin loft is unknown, we can get a reasonable estimate of the launch angle by taking 75% of the effective loft for mid irons, short irons, and wedges, 80% for long irons and fairway woods, or 85% for drivers.

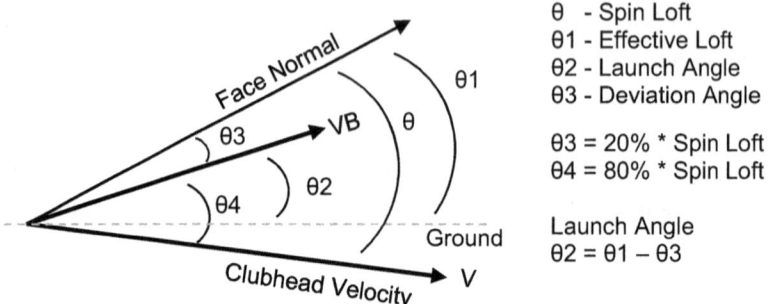

Fig. 5-17 Launch Angle Estimation

Now let's look at a couple of examples.

Example one: for a 45° pitching wedge with 12° forward shaft lean and a -5° attack angle at impact, we know the effective loft is 33° and spin loft is 38°. According to our calculation, the ball's vertical deviation angle is 38° * 20% = 7.6° and its launch angle is therefore:
33° - 7.6° = 25.4°

To do a rough estimation using effective loft only, we get 33° * 75% = 24.75°, which is quite close.

Example two: for a 26° 5-iron with 10° forward shaft lean and a -3° attack angle, the effective loft is 16° and spin loft is 19°. The ball's launch angle is calculated as: 16°- 19° * 20% = 12.2°. To get a rough estimate using effective loft only, we have 16° * 75% = 12°.

In reality, a ball doesn't always achieve pure rolling. This can happen in a drive when a ball, especially a low compression one, is drastically compressed and fails to roll effectively. It can also happen in a wedge shot, where a ball won't stop sliding in time due to a strong spinning vector and poor friction, which can happen when a shot is hit from the rough, a Surlyn-covered ball is used, or the grooves are worn out (more details in Chapter 10 and Chapter 11).

Without pure rolling, the vertical deviation angle will be smaller than the ideal value predicted, and the launch angle will be greater.

SPIN VS. CLUB LOFT

The chart in Fig. 5-18 shows how spinning vector and launch vector change proportionally with the spin loft. With the spin loft at 45°, the spinning vector and launch vector are identical in magnitude, both being 70.7% of the clubhead speed. This is also the point where the relative positions of the two swap. The ratio of VS/V increases more than five times from 15% for a driver to 85% for a wedge. Yet the club speed drops only 25~30%.

Overall, the increase of VS/V drastically outpaces the decrease in clubhead speed as the club loft gets higher. This is why the spin rate typically increases with the club loft, which the spin loft tracks closely. This trend is clearly shown in Table 5-1, which lists PGA tour players' average clubhead speeds and spin rates provided by Trackman.

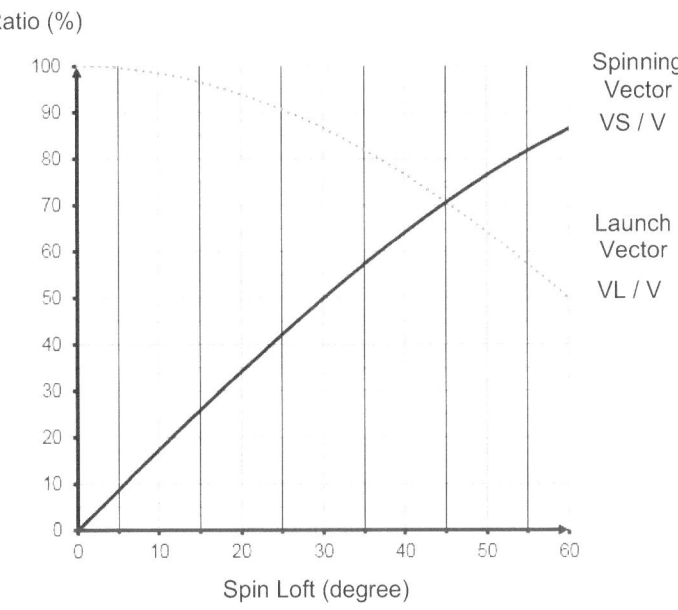

Fig. 5-18 Spinning Vector vs. Spin Loft

Table 5-1
Average Club Speed and Spin Rate in PGA Tour

Club	Clubhead Speed (mph)	Ball Speed (mph)	Spin Rate (rpm)
Driver	112	167	2400-3000
3-wood	107	158	3655
5-wood	103	152	4350
3-iron	98	142	4630
4-iron	96	137	4836
5-iron	94	132	5361
6-iron	92	127	6231
7-iron	90	120	7097
8-iron	87	115	7998
9-iron	85	109	8647
PW	83	102	9304

BACKSPIN: AN INDISPENSABLE ELEMENT IN GOLF

Numerous articles and videos on the internet promise to show golfers the secret about creating backspin. After our discussions of the golf impact, it should be evident by now that backspin is the inevitable outcome of proper ball striking using a lofted club. You don't need any secret move to produce backspin. Just give the ball a solid strike and the club will make that happen. Nonetheless, it is possible to manipulate ball spin rate to a certain degree by using ball striking techniques.

It is amazing how a brief impact in golf is capable of producing a tremendous amount of backspin, which can be over 10,000 rpm for wedges. In other words, a ball can spin more than 167 revolutions in one second, which is phenomenal considering the impact lasts only half a millisecond.

What about topspin? Well, topspin is not something golfers want to deal with except in putting. An airborne golf ball with topspin means disaster, because it will drop quickly like a rock thrown into a swimming pool. With a lofted club, topspin may only happen in a mishit in which the leading edge of the clubface strikes the upper portion of the golf ball.

How to Boost Backspin

Avid golfers always want more backspin on their approach shots. How do we produce stronger backspin so a perfect shot landing on the green won't roll off? By combining the equations shown in Fig. 5-15, we will be able to figure out what determines the spin rate for a ball in pure rolling. The equation below tells us precisely what to do to boost spin rate.

Spin_Rate = 145 * Club_Speed * sin (Spin_Loft)

First and foremost, we want to get the ball as close to pure rolling as possible at the end of impact. Pure rolling means a ball can achieve the maximum spin rate listed in the equation above. For high-loft wedges, pure rolling might not always be possible but we can get the best result by improving the ball-clubface friction, which helps the ball stop sliding sooner and therefore boost spin. This can be achieved by making sure the grooves are clean and in good shape. Also consider using golf balls with soft cover in wedge shots.

Secondly, increase the spin loft, i.e. the angle between clubface normal and swing direction. Spin loft increase can be achieved by using a club with a higher loft, opening the clubface, or simply by hitting down on the ball. Please keep in mind, there would be no change in spin loft if you hit down by 5° but also reduce the effective loft by the same amount in the meantime.

Thirdly, we can boost spin rate by increasing clubhead speed and making solid contact. With everything else being the same, a higher clubhead speed usually produces higher spin. Hitting a 56° sand wedge with a full swing is better than hitting a PW with a half swing if you want more backspin.

Launch Angle vs. Distance

Many golfers have learned in high school physics that a projectile with a given initial speed would travel the longest distance when launched at a 45° angle, as shown in Fig. 5-19. This doesn't seem to match what we see in golf, because a 45° pitch wedge can only delivery half of the distance that a 10° driver can offer. Why is that?

In fact, with the information provided in this book so far we can already find the answer to this question. There are a few reasons.

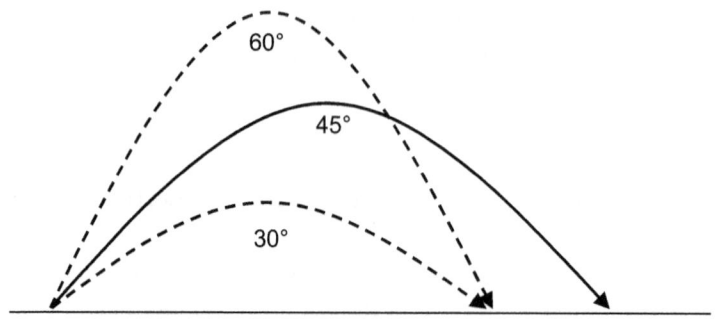

Fig. 5-19 Projectile Trajectories in a Vacuum

First, a golf ball is launched at different speeds by different clubs. Taking a look at Table 5-1 again, we will notice that the average ball speed in a drive is 167 mph among PGA pros, whereas that in a PW shot is only 102 mph. There are two main reasons why a longer club produces higher ball speeds: shaft length and loft. A longer shaft helps produce higher clubhead speeds; and a lower-lofted club distributes more energy in the face normal direction to launch a ball faster.

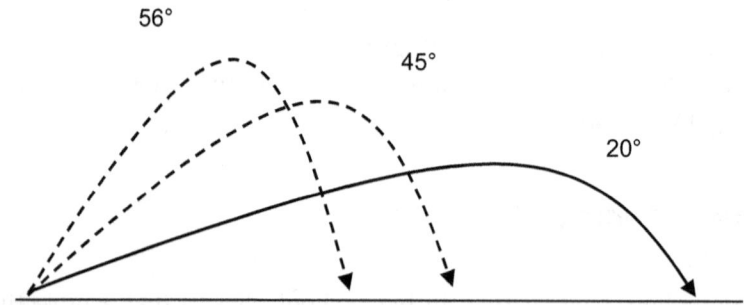

Fig. 5-20 Actual Trajectories in Golf

Secondly, the projectile discussed in the physics textbook is assumed to be in a vacuum, where air resistance and the Magus force don't exist. Air resistance has some impact on a ball's trajectory, but the real game changer is the Magus force. In golf, the Magus force, which increases with the ball speed and spin rate, fights gravity to keep a ball airborne longer so we don't have to use high launch angle to earn flight time. That is why a lower-lofted club, which distributes more energy to the launch vector in the face normal direction, produces higher ball speeds and delivers longer distances, as long as it creates enough backspin.

Of course, there is a limit on how low a ball can launch before it starts to lose distance. The optimal launch angle is approximately between 12° and 16°, depending on the ball design, the launch speed, and the spin rate. Bear in mind, launch angle usually has a different value from the club loft. We can launch a ball at a 14° angle using a 10° driver by changing the attack angle, the impact location, or both.

DISTANCE GAP

A set of well-designed golf clubs is supposed to produce an even distance gap of 10~15 yards between adjacent clubs. Sometimes this task cannot be accomplished by changing loft alone, so designers also have to increase the shaft length of lower-lofted clubs to get higher clubhead speeds. That is why the 4-iron in a traditional set is usually 2~3 inches longer than the PW.

However, difference in club length gives golfers a different feel and forces them to adjust their swing setup. A longer club is usually more difficult to control. Most golfers love hitting their mid and short irons but cannot say the same about the longer ones.

Some club manufacturers, such as Cobra Golf, are now offering single-length irons. For example, the standard length for the KING F9 ONE Length iron set is 37.25", which is the length of a 6-iron in a traditional set. Even though the 4-iron in this ONE Length set has a very strong loft, which is 19.5° instead of the 22~23° in a traditional set, the distance range and gapping still leave much room for improvement, at least for now.

6. Curve Shots

Ben Hogan once said, "You only hit a straight ball by accident." Jack Nicklaus also has a famous quote, "A perfectly straight shot with a big club is a fluke." Indeed, shooting a perfect straight shot is no easy task: both the clubhead velocity and the face normal must be on a vertical plane and pointing to the target. Even the best ball strikers on tour don't make perfect square impact often. Sometime, the situation would even demand a curve shot. It is important that golfers understand what transpires in a non-square impact so they can use different ball flight strategies in the game.

Non-square Strikes

In a non-square strike, the clubhead velocity is not perpendicular to the grooves and thus not in the Y-plane. There are two non-square impact scenarios: the clubface is either open or closed to the clubhead velocity. For simplicity and convenience, we will refer to these two non-square scenarios as *open-face strike* and *closed-face strike* respectively.

It is important to remember that the clubface orientation in these scenarios uses the clubhead velocity, not the target line, as its reference. Sometimes it may appear that we use the target line as the reference, but that is only because the clubhead velocity coincides with the target line in a normal straight shot.

The open-face strike scenario is more commonly seen among high-handicap golfers, whereas the closed-face scenario usually involves more experienced players.

OPEN-FACE STRIKE

In an open-face strike, the clubhead approaches the ball with its heel leading the toe. At impact, the clubhead velocity and the grooves form an angle greater than 90°, as in Fig. 6-1. Or we can say the clubhead velocity points to the golfer side of the Y-plane. To simplify analyses, we will assume the grooves, as well as the club velocity, are parallel to the ground at the moment of impact.

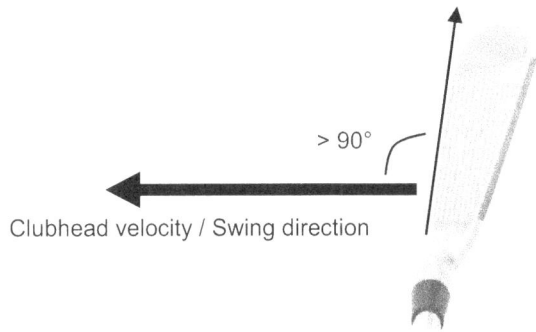

Fig. 6-1 Open-face Strike

Since the clubhead velocity VO (O stands for open) is not perpendicular to the grooves, we can first decompose it into two components on a horizontal plane, as shown in Fig. 6-2. One component, V, is perpendicular to the grooves and the other, VSS, is parallel to them. Here SS stands for sidespin.

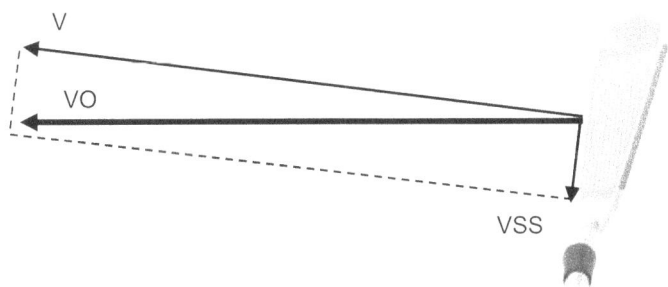

Fig. 6-2 Velocity Decomposition on a Horizontal Plane

Component V is the clubhead velocity in the square strike scenario and it will launch the ball straight ahead with pure backspin (no sidespin). Component VSS is parallel to the grooves and points to the golfer. Similar to how VS produces backspin, this sideways movement of the clubface puts clockwise sidespin on the ball via surface friction.

The clockwise sidespin, according to our previous discussions, will generate a Magnus force pointing away from the golfer and cause a ball to curve right as it travels in the air. For right-handed golfers, such a ball flight is called a fade or a slice, depending on the severity of the curve. Some players, such as Tiger Woods, also use the term "cut shot" for a fade, probably because the swing to produce a fade resembles the cutting motion.

In summary, *striking a ball with the clubface open to the clubhead velocity or swing direction imparts clockwise sidespin to the ball and makes it curve right.* Clubface being open to the clubhead velocity is the primary cause for fade and slice shots.

THE ATTRIBUTES OF A FADE SHOT

Since a club's effective loft increases as the clubface rotates from square to open, the ball flight in a fade shot has the following attributes:
- Higher launch angle
- Higher spin rate
- Shorter distance
- Softer landing

Because the higher launch angle and spin rate allow a ball to land more softly and stop sooner, this type of ball flight can be beneficial for approach shots.

HOW TO HIT A FADE

Golf is full of excitement. There will be situations in which we want to intentionally hit a fade or even a slice. It could be that we need the ball to go around a big tree, or we want the ball to have a softer landing on the green.

From a golfer's perspective, there are two different approaches to hitting a fade. Both are based on the same principle: setting the clubface open to the clubhead velocity at impact.

With the first approach, the golfer sets up for a normal on-plane swing along the baseline but keeps the clubface open to that line, as seen in Fig. 6-3. The baseline is not necessarily the target line, but a reference for alignment.

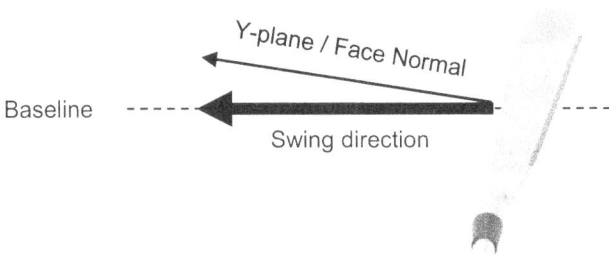

Fig. 6-3 Hitting a Fade with the Clubface Open to Baseline

At impact, the clubhead swings along the baseline and strikes the ball with the clubface open to the swing direction. The ball will launch initially to the right, between the Y-plane and the baseline, and then curve further right as it travels in the air. If the golfer wants the fade shot to land on a target, the baseline must point to the left of the target.

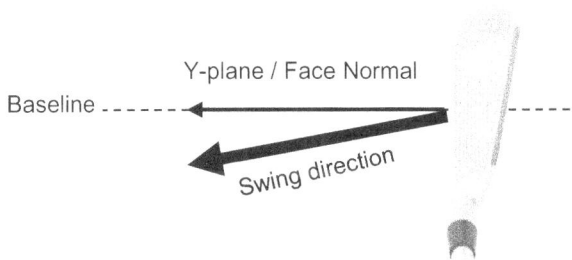

Fig. 6-4 Hitting a fade with an Outside-in Swing

With the second approach, the golfer keeps the clubface square to the baseline and swings along an outside-to-inside path (Fig. 6-4). Initially, the ball will launch slightly to the left, between the Y-plane and the baseline, and then curve right as it travels in the air.

In both approaches, the golf ball would see the same thing: the clubhead moving in with its heel ahead of its toe. Both approaches will create clockwise sidespin, and therefore cause the ball to curve right in the air.

However, the swing executions do feel different to the golfer. With the second approach, turning the clubface open at impact also increases the effective loft.

One benefit of the first approach is that the golfer doesn't need to change his swing mechanics and is less prone to inconsistency. When the situation calls for it, the two approaches can be combined to produce a big slice.

How to Fix a Slice

More often than not, a slice isn't part of the game plan. It happens by accident and usually causes trouble and frustration. Don't we all hate accidental slice shots? The fundamental cause of slice, as we have pointed out, is the deviation of clubhead velocity from the Y-plane. In other words, the clubface is open to the clubhead swing direction at impact. For drivers and fairway woods, a slice can also be caused by the gear effect, a phenomenon we will discuss in Chapter Nine.

In actual shot execution, a slice can be caused by one or more of the following specific issues.
- An outside-to-inside swing path
- Clubface being open at impact
- Gear effect from a heel shot

Outside-to-inside Swing Path

The outside-to-inside swing path is by far the most common cause for slice among beginners and high-handicap golfers. In theory, an outside-in swing path by itself is not enough to produce a slice, but in reality it almost always does for beginners. Even if the clubface is square to the target line at impact, it is still open to the swing direction and will produce a slice. Only by closing the clubface there can be a chance of hitting a straight pull shot. Without fixing the outside-in swing path, it is impossible to hit a straight shot that goes toward the target.

An outside-to-inside swing path is typically the result of an untrained downswing movement. Due to the anatomical limitations of the human body, a club at the top of a full backswing sits above the striking plane, which is the plane a club should travel on below the waist line in order to produce a straight target-seeking shot. Detailed discussions on this topic can be found in *Decoding the Golf Swing Plane*.

Fig. 6-5 Outside-to-inside Downswing Move

From the top of a full swing, a beginner tends to get too active with his upper body and attack the ball directly by swinging the club down in front of his body because it feels easy and natural. He will end up cutting the club across the striking plane from outside to inside. The picture in Fig. 6-5 shows such a move and was extracted from a swing video recorded during a game. This is also known as the "over the top" move because the club approaches the ball from above the striking plane.

To get rid of the notorious outside-to-inside swing path, a golfer must learn to lower the club onto the striking plane during the first half of the downswing. This is a signature move among professional players, as shown in Fig.6-6. With the club back on plane, the golfer can then accelerate the clubhead aggressively to strike the ball.

Fig. 6-6　On-plane Downswing Move

Clubface Open at Impact

An on-plane swing only guarantees that the clubhead velocity would point in the target direction at impact. Since a straight shot requires the clubface being square to the clubhead velocity, a golfer with a perfect on-plane swing can still hit a slice if the clubface is open at impact. This can be a problem for both beginners and experienced players. Clubface being open can be the result of incorrect wrist action, which fails to square the clubface at impact.

A good drill for wrist action is to practice swing with the trail hand moved down the shaft so the two hands are about four inches apart. Swing the club using this hockey style grip for a few minutes and you will get the right feel.

It is also quite common that a beginner's wrist action only square the clubface for a very short moment. Ben Hogan, being a great ball striker, is said to be able to keep the clubface square for a longer period of time by bowing his left wrist, and therefore boosted his chance of hitting straight shots.

The Gear Effect

Even with an on-plane swing and a square clubface at impact, golfers are still not completely out of the woods.

When a ball is struck on the heel of a driver or fairway wood, it could curve from left to right due to a phenomenon called the gear effect, which will be discussed in more details in Chapter Nine. As a good practice, golfers should always be mindful of impact locations when diagnosing ball flight issues.

CLOSED-FACE STRIKE

In a closed-face strike, the clubhead approaches the ball with its toe leading the heel right before impact. The clubhead velocity and the grooves on the clubface form an angle smaller than 90° at the moment of impact (Fig. 6-7).

In this scenario, the clubhead velocity is no longer inside the Y-plane; it points to the toe side instead.

As usual, we assume the grooves, as well as the club velocity, are parallel to the ground at the moment of impact. The analysis process will still be the same even if these conditions are not met. However, these assumptions do make things simpler and easier to understand in the beginning.

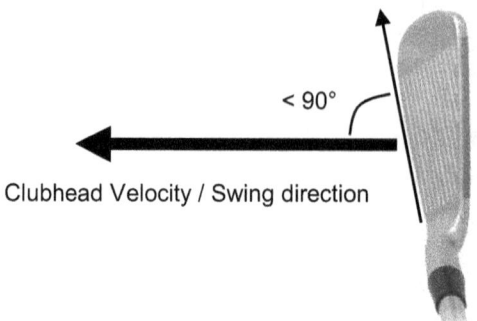

Fig. 6-7 Closed-face Strike

In this case, the clubhead velocity VC (C stands for closed) is not perpendicular to the grooves. We can decompose it into two components on a horizontal plane (Fig. 6-8). One component, V, is perpendicular to the grooves and the other, VSS, is parallel to them.

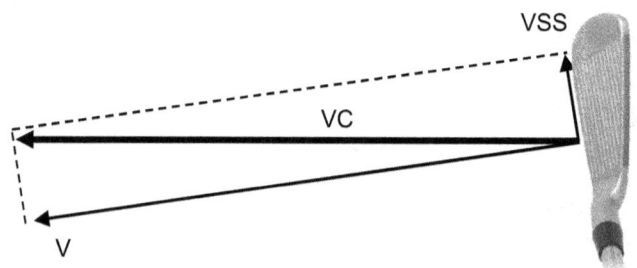

Fig. 6-8 Velocity Decomposition on the Horizontal Plane

Component V is the clubhead velocity discussed in the square strike scenario and it launches the ball straight with pure backspin (no sidespin). Component VSS is parallel to the grooves and points away from the golfer. This sideways movement of the clubface applies friction to the ball and creates counterclockwise sidespin, which causes the ball to curve from right to left as it travels in the air. For right-handed golfers, this ball flight is called a draw or a hook, depending on how severe the curve is.

Curve Shots

THE ATTRIBUTES OF A DRAW SHOT

Since a club's effective loft decreases when its clubface rotates from square to closed, the ball flight in a draw has the following attributes:
- Lower launch angle
- Lower spin rate
- Longer distance
- More rolling after landing

Therefore, if you want a shot to go a few extra yards than your normal club distance, consider hitting a draw.

HOW TO HIT A DRAW

There are also two approaches to hitting a draw. With the first approach, the golfer sets up for a normal on-plane swing along the baseline but keeps the clubface closed to this line (Fig. 6-9). At impact, the clubhead swings along the baseline and strikes the ball with the clubface closed. The ball will launch to the left, between the Y-plane and the baseline, and then curve further left as it travels in the air.

To use the first approach, the baseline should be adjusted accordingly so it points to the right side of the intended target. The amount of adjustment can be determined through practice.

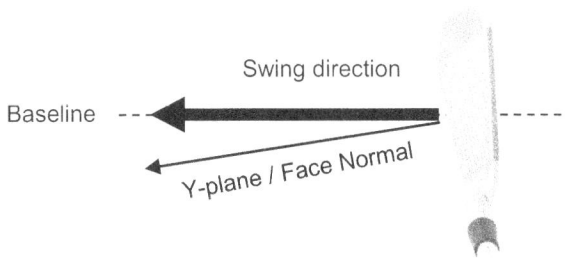

Fig. 6-9 Hitting a Draw with the Clubface Closed

65

With the second approach, the golfer keeps the clubface square to the baseline but swings from inside to outside. At impact, the clubhead velocity points right and the clubface is closed to the swing direction. The ball will launch slightly to the right of the baseline initially and then curve left as it travels in the air.

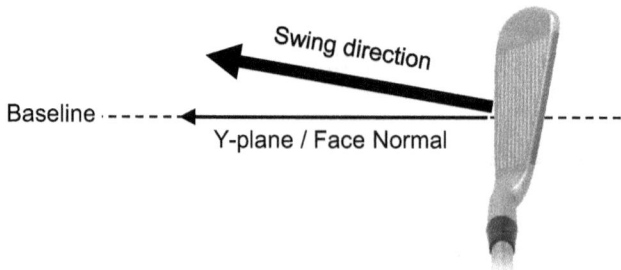

Fig. 6-10 Hitting a Draw with Inside-out Swing Direction

In both approaches, the golf ball sees the same: the clubhead moving in with its toe leading the heel. However, the swing executions do feel different to the golfer. With the first approach, getting the clubface closed at impact also reduces the effective loft; yet this isn't the case with the second method.

The benefit of the first approach is that the golfer doesn't have to change his swing mechanics and is less prone to inconsistency.

LAUNCH DIRECTION

In golf, *Launch direction* is used to describe a ball's initial path from a bird's eye view. It tells us whether a shot starts straight, left, or right. Alternatively, launch direction can be called the *horizontal launch angle*, which is a less confusing and more appropriate technically.

When talking about launch direction, we usually use the target line as the reference. Launch direction is defined as the angle between a ball's initial trajectory and the target line from the bird's eye view, as shown in Fig. 6-11. Among popular launch monitors, launch direction pointing to the right (left) of the target line is described using a positive (negative) angle.

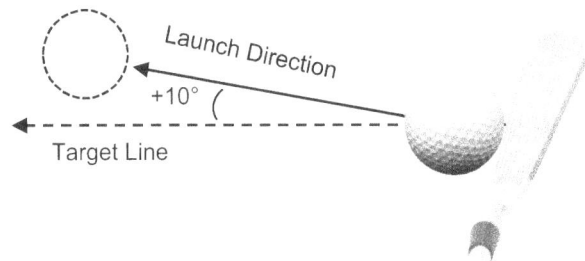

Fig. 6-11 Launch Direction

Launch direction is an important parameter in golf ball flight. To successfully plan and shape shots, golfers should understand how it is related to clubface orientation and swing direction.

In the old days, people commonly believed that a ball would launch along the clubhead's swing direction at impact. There were also people who thought launch direction is where the clubface points to at impact. In fact, either may appear to be true in specific scenarios but neither is technically accurate.

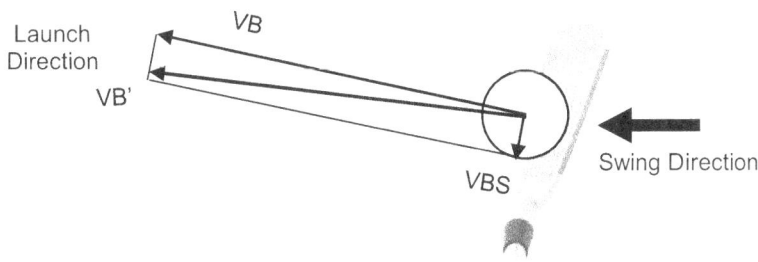

Fig. 6-12 Actual Launch Direction in a Fade

In Chapter Five we discussed how spinning vector VS could impart both backspin and translational velocity to a ball. For the same reason, the sideways movement of clubhead (VSS) will impart sidespin and translational velocity (VBS) to a ball.

This sideways translational velocity VBS, when combined with the ball's velocity from a square strike (VB), produces the total ball launch velocity VB', as shown in Fig. 6-12. Since VB is inside the Y-plane, a non-zero VBS will cause VB' to point slightly away from the Y-plane. According to our discussions in Chapter Five, VB itself can be decomposed into two components, VBN and VBD. Therefore, a ball's total launch velocity in a curve shot (VB') consists of three components, which are VBN (normal to clubface), VBD (parallel to clubface and pointing downward), and VBS (parallel to the grooves and pointing sideways).

VBS is not zero in a non-square strike. Assuming pure rolling is achieved, the magnitude of VBS can be calculated using the following equation, where VBS and VSS both are in mph.

VBS = VSS * 2/7

If a ball fails to achieve pure rolling, VBS will be lower and so will the sidespin rate. When this happens, the sideways deviation of VB' from the Y-plane will also decrease.

This sideways deviation of VB' from the Y-plane, also called the *horizontal deviation angle*, for a ball in pure rolling can be calculated, like what we did for the vertical direction. We will skip the detailed calculation and offer a general guideline here instead.

With pure rolling achieved, from a bird's eye view, the horizontal deviation angle of the launch trajectory from the Y-plane is about 20%~30% of the angle between the clubhead velocity and the Y-plane, depending on the weight of the clubhead. It is approximately 20% for drivers, fairway woods, and long irons; 25% for mid and short irons; and 30% for wedges. For a quick estimation, we can use 25% across the board.

For example, an 8-iron strikes a ball with its face open to the swing direction by 20°. The launch direction's horizontal deviation angle is about 5° (20 x 25% = 5°) off the Y-plane, as shown in Fig. 6-13. Assuming the swing direction coincides with the target line at impact, the launch direction will be 15° to the right of the target line. Of course, 20° is a massive face angle and is only used here to make a point. If the clubface is open by only 8°, then the ball will launch in a direction that is only 2° off the Y-plane and 6° off the target line. Since 2° is a very small angle, many people might feel the ball actually launches along the Y-plane, or where the clubface is pointing.

To summarize, the launch direction, or the horizontal launch angle, is mainly determined by the orientation of the clubface. The influence from swing direction is heavily discounted and down to about 25%, which will be even less if a ball doesn't reach pure rolling before launch.

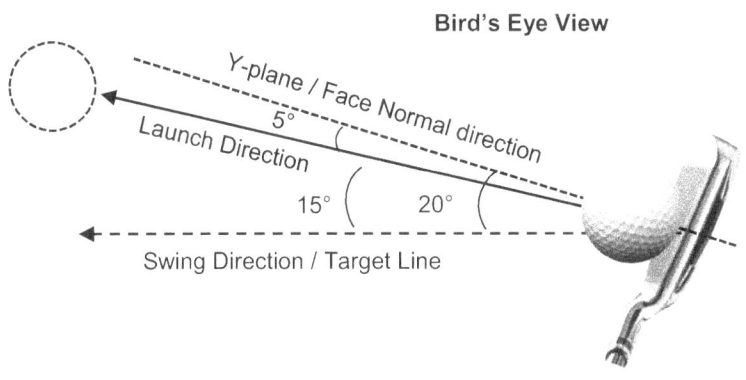

Fig. 6-13 Launch Direction

Spin Axis

So far we have looked at backspin and sidespin separately. This is a "divide and conquer" approach that makes it easier to understand the role of each type of spin and its relationship with the clubhead velocity.

In real-world ball flight, backspin and sidespin don't exist separately; they show up as one combined spin motion. The axis of a pure backspin is parallel to the horizontal plane, whereas that of pure sidespin is perpendicular to it (Fig. 6-14). The combination of

69

the two will produce a tilted axis, which is neither parallel nor perpendicular to the horizontal plane.

The diagrams in Fig. 6-14 show what an actual ball spin may look like. For right-handed golfers, the mixture of backspin and clockwise sidespin is the fade spin, whose axis tilts down. In contrast, the combination of backspin and counterclockwise sidespin becomes the draw spin, whose axis tilts up.

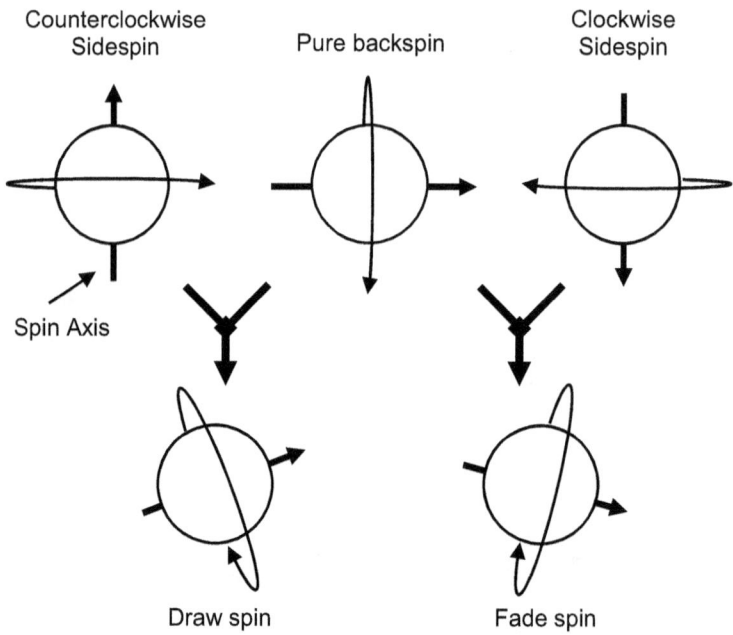

Fig. 6-14 Actual Ball Spin

In popular launch monitors, a spin axis is assigned a zero degree angle for pure backspin, a positive angle for a fade spin, and a negative one for a draw spin. The tilt angle of spin axis is determined by the ratio of sidespin to backspin. For instance, with equal amounts of backspin and clockwise sidespin, the spin axis tilts down at a + 45° angle. According to Trackman, a ball will curve 0.7% off the target line for every degree of spin axis tilt.

WHY IS IT MUCH EASIER TO SLICE WITH DRIVERS?

Due to its small spin loft, a driver produces a much lower spin rate than a wedge. The typical spin rate is 2000~3000 rpm for a driver, whereas that of a wedge can reach 9000~12000 rpm.

Let's look at some numbers. For a drive with a backspin rate of 2500 rpm, a clockwise sidespin rate of 600 rpm can tilt the spin axis by 13.5° and cause a severe slice. Yet for a wedge shot with a backspin rate of 9500 rpm, the same amount of sidespin can only tilt the spin axis by 3.6°, which will only produce a very subtle fade. In addition, the ball in a drive travels a much longer distance than in a wedge shot and distance will further amplify the effect of sidespin. This is why we can drastically open the face of a sand wedge in ball striking without worrying about slice.

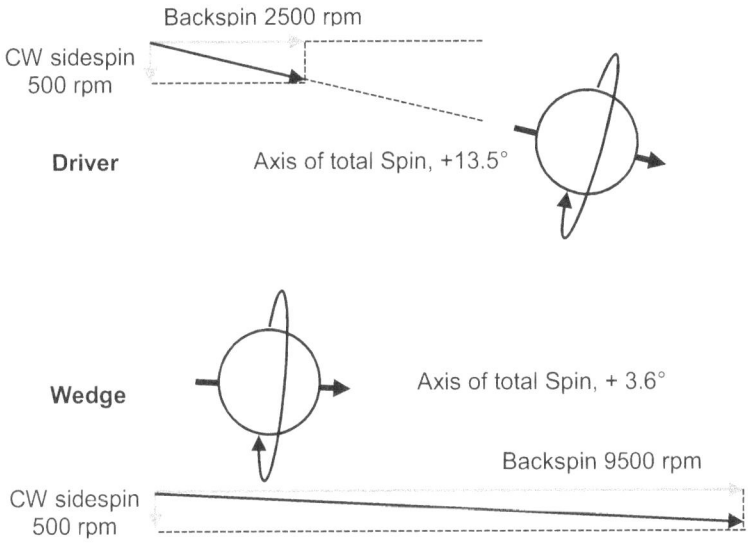

Fig. 6-15 Spin Axis Tilt Angle

Ball Flight Summary

The following diagrams summarize the relationship between swing direction and clubface orientation (Y-plane) at impact.

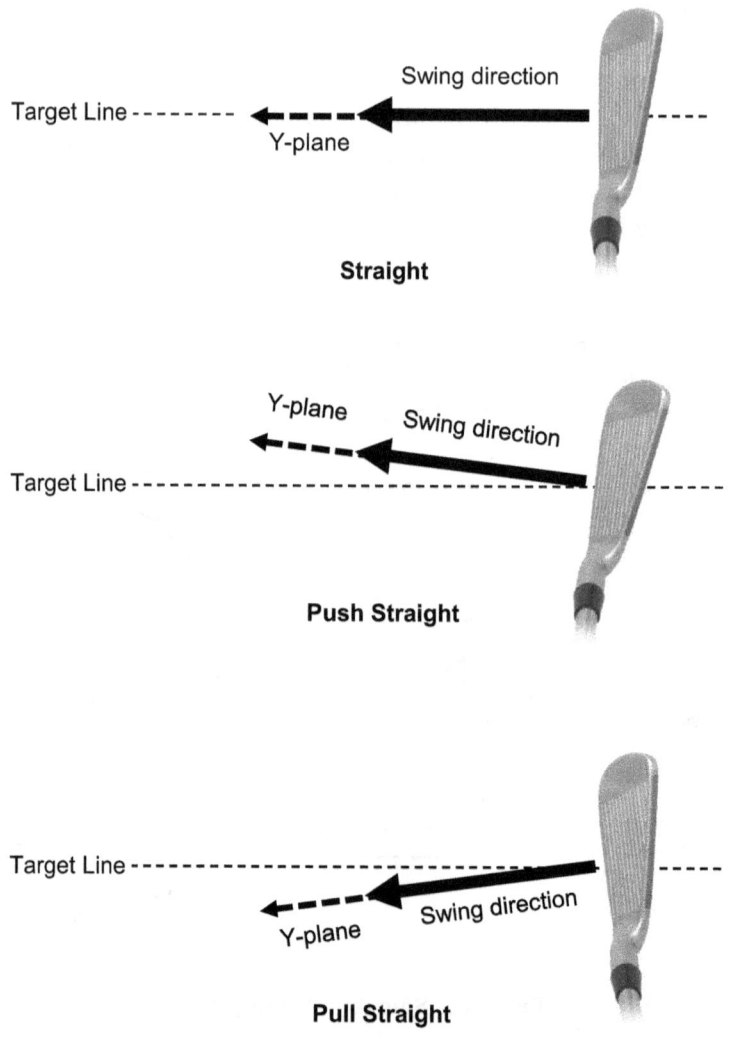

Fig. 6-16   Straight Shots

Curve Shots

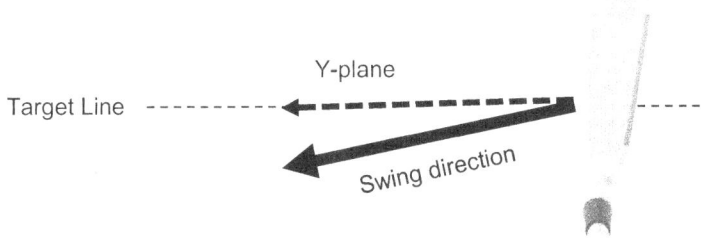

Fade / Slice

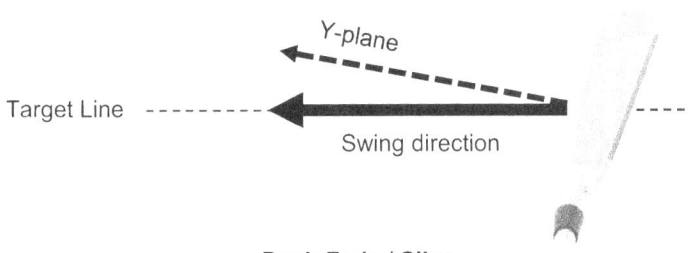

Push Fade / Slice

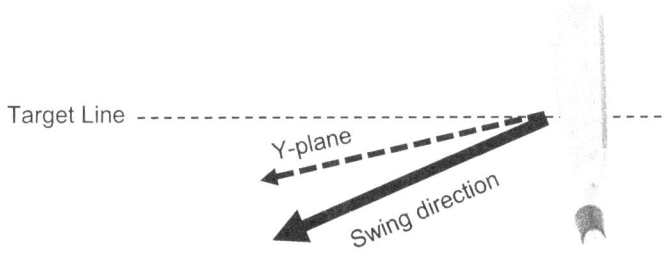

Pull Fade / Slice

Fig. 6-17   Fade / Slice Shots

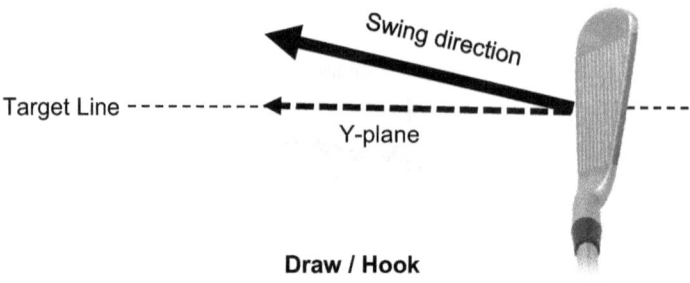

Draw / Hook

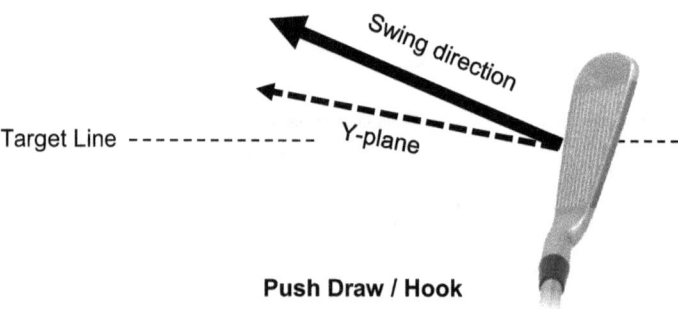

Push Draw / Hook

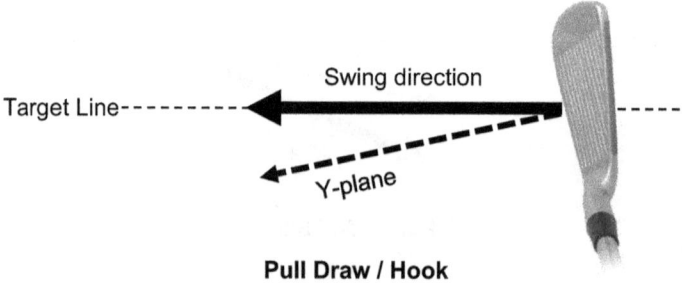

Pull Draw / Hook

Fig. 6-18   Draw / Hook Shots

7. D-PLANE

In the last decade, D-plane has somehow become a hot topic in the golf community. Some people have claimed that it is "the secret of ball flight" and "the impact theory that is changing the way you swing." Tons of articles and videos can be found on the internet talking about this seemingly sophisticated and confusing term.

Many golfers have diligently dug into the D-plane theory in the hope of finding a magical solution to the swing challenges they have been dealing with. Unfortunately, many of the materials online are making this concept more complicated than it really is, or claiming it to be something that it is not.

WHAT ON EARTH IS THIS D-PLANE?

It appears that the term D-plane is first used by Theodore Jorgensen, a physics professor at the University of Nebraska, in his book *The Physics of Golf*. The definition of D-plane given in his book is as follows:

"The normal to the clubface and the line along which the clubhead is moving at impact intersect at the ball and therefore determine a plane. The line along which the ball leaves the clubhead also lies in this plane. We shall call this plane the D plane because it is descriptive of the collision between the clubhead and the ball."

The "normal to the clubface" is a straight line perpendicular to the clubface, i.e. the face normal. The "line along which the clubhead is moving" is the same line representing the clubhead velocity vector. Strictly speaking, both lines pass through the CG of the clubhead and thus won't intersect at the ball.

D-PLANE IN A SQUARE STRIKE

Fig. 7-1 shows the D-plane in a square strike, where the clubhead velocity is perpendicular to the grooves. Please bear in mind that D-plane is not limited to the shaded area, but extends to infinity. In a square strike, D-plane is perpendicular to the grooves, and therefore coincides with the Y-plane. In Fig. 7-1, the D-plane is also shown from a different perspective where the clubface is laid flat.

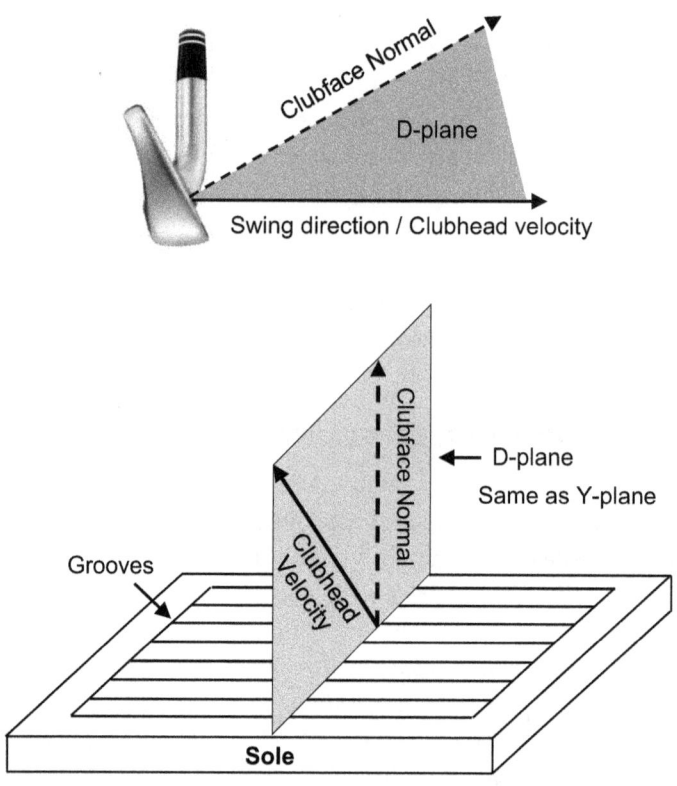

Fig. 7-1 D-plane in a Square Strike

In a square strike, we assume the sole of the club sits properly so the grooves are parallel to ground. The D-plane is therefore a vertical plane and appears to be a straight line from the bird's eye view (Fig. 7-2). The ball will launch off on the D-plane with pure backspin. It will fly straight to the destination and stay on this vertical D-plane during the entire flight, unless blown away by the wind. The spin axis is perpendicular to the D-plane.

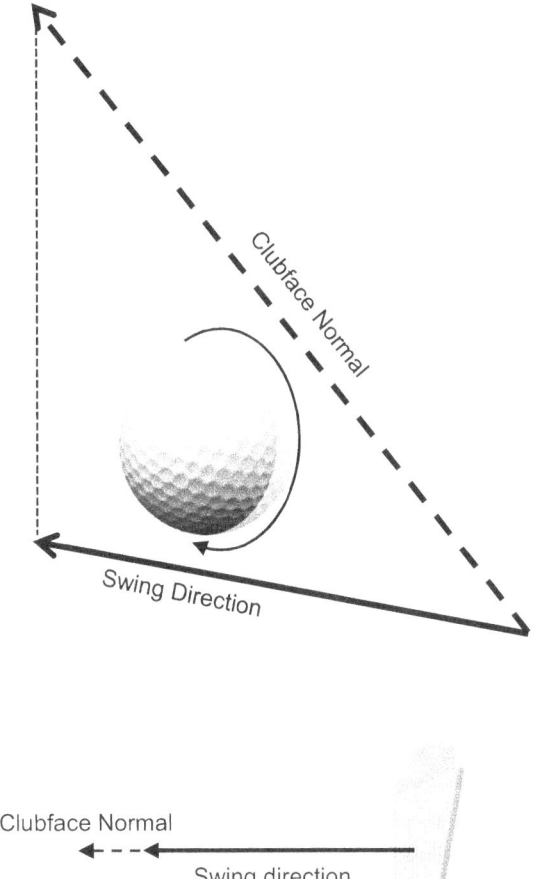

Fig. 7-2 D-plane in a Square Strike

D-PLANE IN A NON-SQUARE STRIKE

In a non-square strike, clubhead velocity points sideways and is not perpendicular to the grooves. The D-plane is still perpendicular to the clubface since it contains the clubface normal, but is no longer perpendicular to the grooves, as shown in Fig. 7-3.

The ball will launch off on this tilted D-plane initially, between the clubhead velocity and the clubface normal but closer to the latter. However, the ball doesn't stay on the D-plane for long because soon the gravity will pull it off. The spin axis is perpendicular to the D-plane, but only in the beginning.

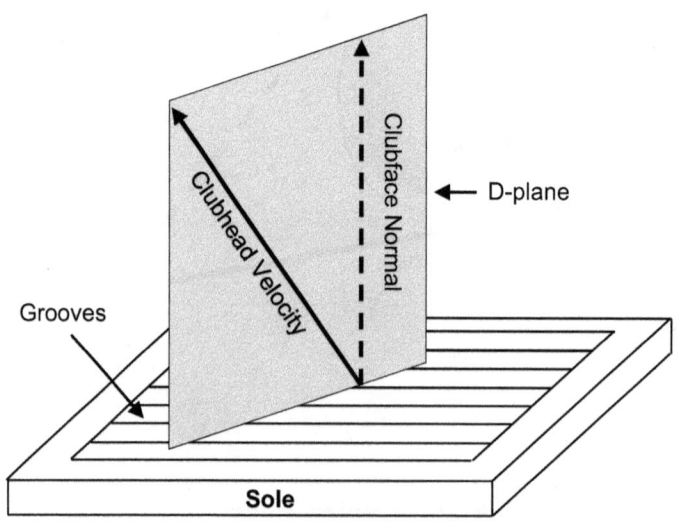

Fig. 7-3 D-plane in a Closed-face Strike

D-plane

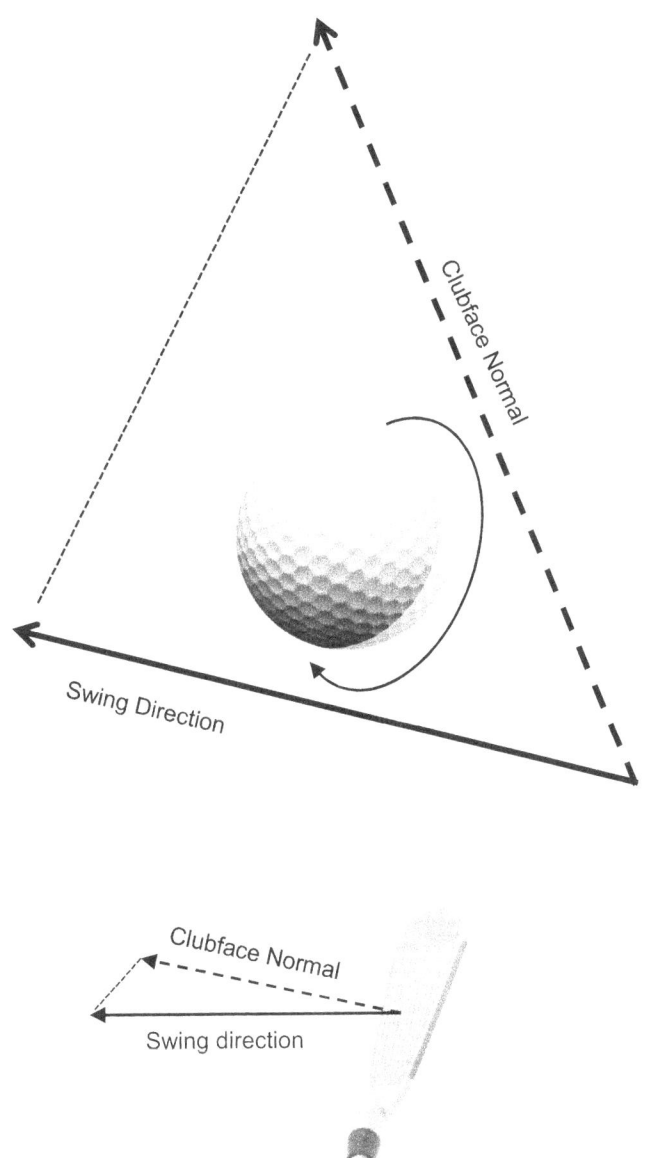

Fig. 7-4 D-plane in An Open-face Strike

THE ESSENCE OF D-PLANE

D-plane might not be the solution to your swing problems, but it has some interesting meanings behind it. We will again use a metal block to model an iron club (Fig. 7-5). The block is laid flat so the lines can be better seen.

Now let's take a look at the square strike scenario (Fig. 7-5). The clubhead velocity is perpendicular to the grooves and can be decomposed into two components along the face normal and face parallel directions. Since this decomposition rectangle contains the clubface normal and clubhead velocity, it is on the D-plane! In other words, the D-plane is the decomposition plane.

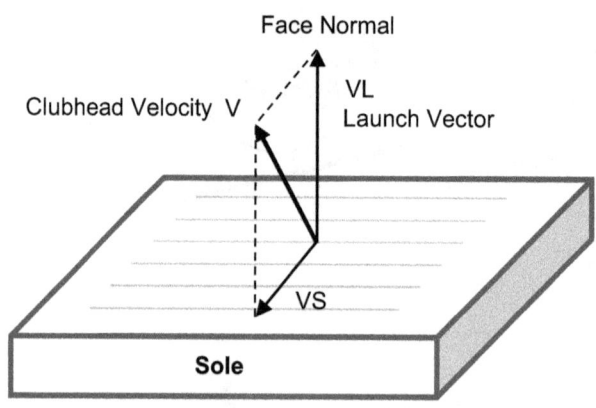

Fig. 7-5 D-plane for a Square Strike

Because spin is driven by VS through the work of friction, the spin equator rotates within the D-plane and the spin axis is thus perpendicular to the same plane.

VBD and VBN are also in the D-plane, so is the ball's total velocity VB. Therefore, the ball will launch off on the D-plane, with its spin axis perpendicular to it. If we keep the grooves parallel to the ground at impact, the D-plane will be a vertical plane, and the ball will travel on this plane until it hits the ground.

For a non-square strike, we can also decompose the clubhead velocity along the face normal and face parallel directions, as shown in Fig. 7-6. Since the decomposition rectangle contains both clubface normal and clubhead velocity, it is on the D-plane!

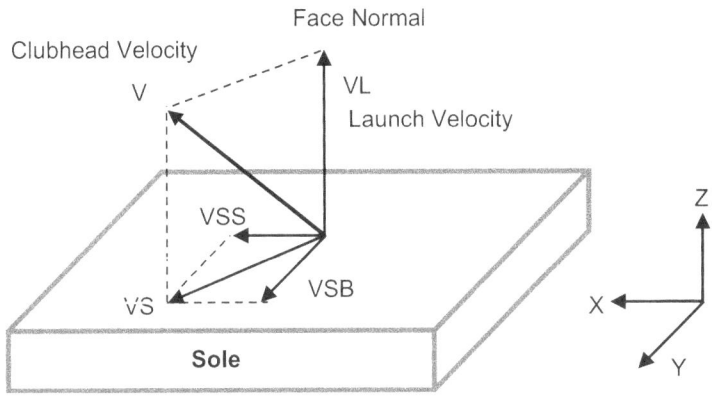

Fig. 7-6 D-plane for a Non-square Strike

In this case, the spinning vector VS is not perpendicular to the grooves. It causes the ball to spin with a tilted spin axis. Just like in a square strike, the spin axis is also perpendicular to the D-plane. This tilted spin is the combination of backspin and sidespin.

We can further decompose VS into two sub-components. One is VSB, which is perpendicular to the grooves and responsible for the backspin; the other is VSS, which is parallel to the grooves and responsible for the sidespin.

The decomposition order here is different from what we did in Chapter Six. The order doesn't matter. Regardless, the final results are the same once we decompose the clubhead velocity down to the three components in the X, Y, Z directions.

In a non-square strike, the spin axis is only perpendicular to the D-plane at the moment of launch. Due to the influence of gravity, a ball in a non-square strike will soon fall off the tilted D-plane as it travels in the air. A curve shot is made possible by the combined action of gravity and sideways Magnus force. Without gravity, a ball with a tilted spin would continue traveling on the D-plane.

Now we can see that D-plane is essentially the decomposition plane since it is where we decompose the clubhead velocity into launch and spinning vectors. The latter determines the initial direction of the spin axis.

In a hypothetical scenario where the club velocity is perfectly perpendicular to the clubface, the spinning vector will be zero and the launch vector will be identical to the clubhead velocity. This is actually the perpendicular collision discussed in Chapter Five. In this case, the "D-plane" is reduced to a straight line and the ball doesn't spin at all.

Summary

The D-plane is nothing magical or mysterious. It does offer golfers an easy way to determine the initial spin orientation and to estimate the initial launch trajectory, but doesn't provide any quantitative information on the spin or launch. The vector decomposition technique discussed in this book is far more accurate and informative for golfers who want to truly understand ball flight.

D-plane certainly is not a magical pill for swing problems. It may help people understand ball flight a little better but won't offer any specific guidance on swing improvement. If you want to better understand the ball-club interaction, vector decomposition is a much better tool. It is not difficult at all, as long as you know how to draw some rectangles.

8. Solid Contact

The ball flight discussions we have had so far are based on one important premise, which assumes a ball is struck on the sweet spot of the clubface. In such a shot, the impact feels sweet, solid, and effortless. Golfers would call this a solid shot and say the club has made solid contact with the ball. But what is the definition of solid contact from Isaac Newton's point of view?

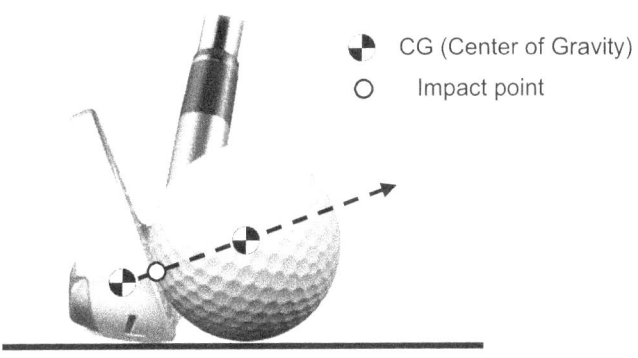

Fig. 8-1 Solid Contact

To make solid contact, the clubhead's CG, ball's CG, and impact point should be on a straight line, which coincides with the face normal (Fig. 8-1). The impact force in the face normal direction points at the ball's CG and produces no torque. Likewise, the reaction force from the ball also points at the clubhead CG and won't cause any unpleasant clubhead twist as the torque is also zero.

With solid contact, the kinetic energy transferred to the ball is maximized, and the ball achieves the highest speed possible for the given clubhead speed and loft. A solid strike delivers a special feel, which many golfers find addictive.

THE IMPORTANCE OF MAKING SOLID CONTACT

The impact location on the clubface is the determining factor for shot quality. A poor shot is most likely related to an off-center impact. Without solid contact, the ball flight rules discussed earlier do not necessarily apply, and the ball trajectory is hard to predict.

In an off-center impact, the reaction force a ball exerting back on the clubhead produces a torque and causes the head to twist around its CG. The clubhead twisting not only compromises kinetic energy transfer but also causes ball flight to deviate from its normal patterns. In addition, it will send an unpleasant shock to the hands holding the club. In the end, a ball's launch data and flight trajectory are all negatively affected. According to Callaway Golf, *impact location on a driver has much more influence on launch angle and backspin than the club's loft.*

It is not uncommon for an average golfer to miss the sweet spot by an inch or two in a drive. Given the same clubhead speed, an off-center impact can easily cost 10~30 yards in distance. Worse yet, an off-center shot can produce undesirable abnormal launch parameters, making it difficult to get valid feedback from ball flight.

Being able to consistently catch a ball on the sweet spot of the clubface is a vital skill and the first step in total ball flight control.

WHERE IS THE SWEET SPOT?

In a solid shot, the impact location on the clubface is called the sweet spot because the shot feels pure and sweet. It is apparent that the location of the sweet spot is associated with the CG of the clubhead. If we draw a line perpendicular to the clubface via the clubhead's CG, the sweet spot is where the line intersects the face.

The location of the CG is affected by the shape and weight distribution of the clubhead. For example, the CG of a game improvement iron clubhead, which usually features a wider sole (thus more weight on the bottom), is lower than that of a blade. This is why an average golfer, who often catches the ball on the lower part of the clubface, will experience improved shot quality with a game improvement iron.

An object's CG is not necessarily located within its body. For instance, a boomerang's CG is outside of its physical structure (Fig. 8-2). In general, the CG of a driver is located within its body. The CG of a blade iron can be very close to the clubface, whereas that of a cavity-back iron is farther behind the clubface and much lower.

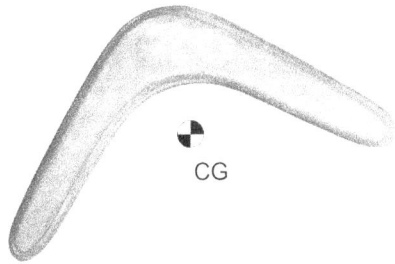

Fig. 8-2 The CG of a Boomerang

While locating the CG of a club may take some work, figuring out the location of the sweet spot is much easier. The quickest way to find the sweet spot is by experiments. Gently hold a club's grip end using the thumb and index fingers so it can swing freely, then tap the clubface using a small hammer. When striking the toe or heel of the clubface, you can see and feel the clubhead twisting because a torque, which tends to make an object rotate around its CG, is produced by the off-center impact. The impact sound is dull, hollow, and obnoxious. With the hammer striking the sweet spot, the entire clubhead would move back without twist, and the sound of impact is solid, crispy, and pleasant.

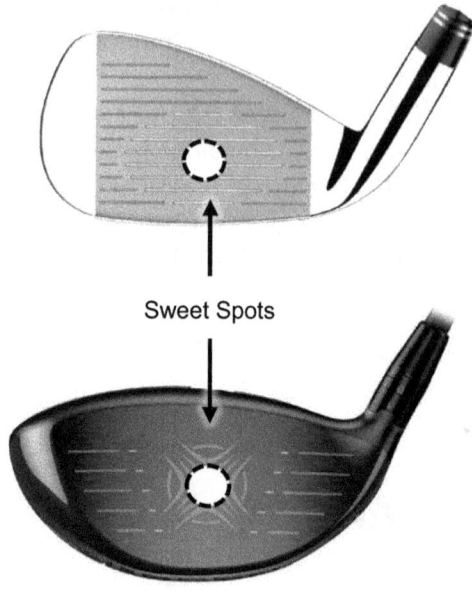

Fig. 8-3 Sweet Spot Locations

The iron shown in Fig. 8-3 has an oval marking on its clubface and the center of the oval is the sweet spot. A shot with the ball impact marking within the oval will produce a decent result.

MAKING SOLID CONTACT WITH AN IRON

To hit solid iron shots, we must first understand how irons are designed and how they are supposed to be used.

Wedges, short irons, and even mid irons typically come with a positive bounce angle, which is shown in Fig. 8-4. That means the leading edge of the clubface is above the ground when the club is in the neutral shaft position. Keep in mind, how much the leading edge is above the ground is not solely determined by the bounce angle, but also by the location of the sole's lowest point. In recent years, more wedge manufacturers are offering multiple bounce angles for each loft option. Typically, each bounce angle is offered with a particular type of grind, which specifies the contour profile of the sole. For example, Callaway offers three bounce/grind options for its 56° wedges: 8°/C, 10°/S, and 12°/W. The leading edge ground clearance for each option is different. A golfer can choose the bounce/grind based how he typically hits wedge shots.

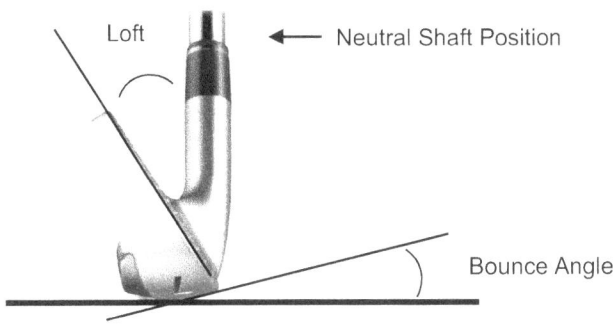

Fig. 8-4 Bounce Angle

Typically, the bounce angle of an iron increases with the loft. Taking a popular iron set from a leading brand as an example, the bounce angle is 1° for the 4-iron, 2° for the 6-iron, 4° for the 8-iron, and 6° for the pitching wedge. A long iron usually has a very small or even a negative bounce angle, and its leading edge is quite close to the ground even in the neutral shaft position.

When we set up with a short or mid-iron and keep its shaft in the neutral position, the contact point between the ball and the clubface is way below the sweet spot and therefore not on the straight line with the two CGs (Fig. 8-5). As the loft of the iron increases, the ball contact point moves further down on the clubface. The increased bounce angle only makes the situation worse.

It is quite difficult to produce a solid iron shot with the shaft in the neutral position at impact, especially on tight lies. This shaft position might produce an acceptable shot when the ball is sufficiently elevated (by grasses or a tee), or in chipping where we don't need high ball speeds. Beyond these, the neutral shaft position makes it difficult or impossible to hit solid iron shots. Unfortunately, this impact position is very common among average golfers. That is why beginners love to see their balls sitting on the first cut rough. In contrast, good ball strikers like Tiger Woods and Phil Mickelson can hit solid shots from a concrete cart path.

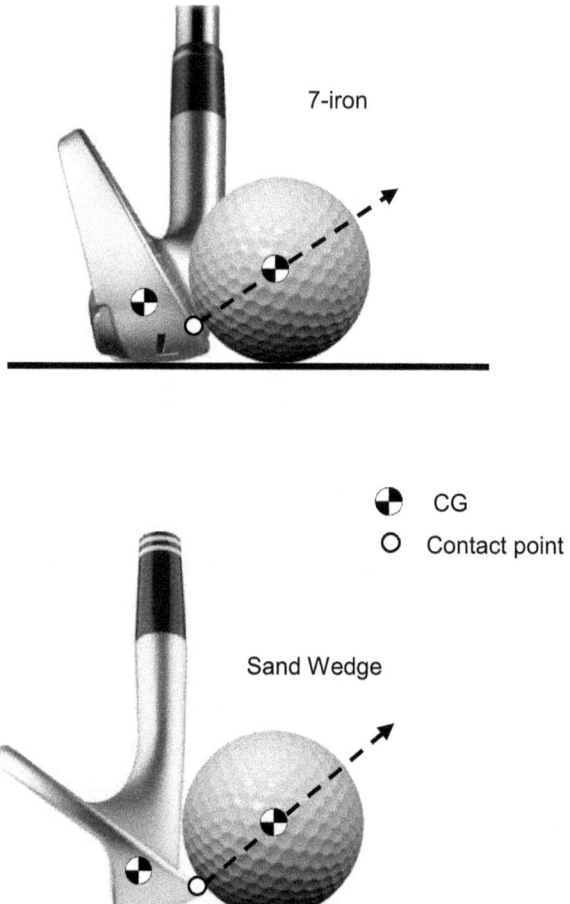

Fig. 8-5 Contact Points with Neutral Shaft Position

If we press the handle toward the target and let the shaft lean forward, the leading edge of the clubface will move closer to and even touch the ground (Fig. 8-6). In the meantime, the contact point moves up and gets closer to the sweet spot. *In fact, an iron, especially a mid or short iron, is designed to strike a ball with its shaft leaning forward.* Only when a golfer achieves such an impact position can he produce pure solid iron shots consistently.

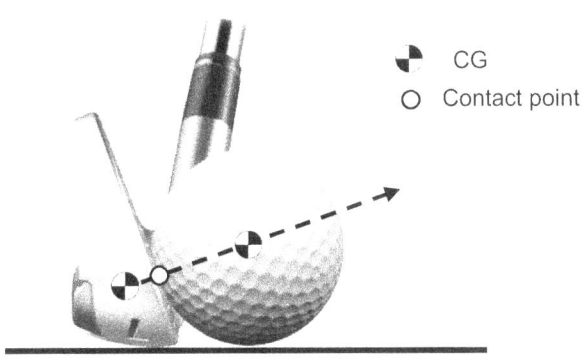

Fig. 8-6 Shaft Leaning Forward

Why is an iron designed to strike a ball with its shaft leaning forward? There are multiple benefits from the perspective of physics.

First, this position allows the impact location to move higher on the clubface so club designers can move the sweet spot higher and closer to clubface center where the spring effect is the strongest.

Secondly, we want the clubhead to catch the ball first because making contact with the ground or grass before impact kills clubhead speed. A downward strike has a much better chance of making clean and solid contact when the ball is on the ground. A forward leaning shaft makes it easier to execute downward striking and is also the natural outcome of a well-sequenced high-speed swing.

Thirdly, when an iron is designed to strike a ball with the shaft leaning forward, its leading edge can be trimmed off to move the impact location higher. Since only a small amount of metal is removed from the edge, the CG location won't change much. This essentially moves the leading edge closer to the sweet spot, making it easier to hit solid shots, especially for wedges and short irons.

Things are slightly different for long irons. Due to their small loft angles, the contact point is much higher and closer to the sweet spot in the neutral shaft position, so it is possible to hit solid shots without drastic forward shaft lean, or at all. That is why good players can "sweep" the long irons, meaning the club travels horizontally at impact.

Regardless of the club used, teeing a ball up always increases the chance of making clean and solid contact. That is exactly why Jack Nicklaus recommended using a tee whenever it was allowed.

MAKING SOLID CONTACT WITH A DRIVER

Drivers are mainly used for tee shots, where a ball is usually supported by a tee and has sufficient ground clearance. This makes it much easier for the sweet spot of a driver to reach the ball. Technically there is no need to hit down on the ball or lean the shaft forward.

The sweet spot of a driver is around the center of the clubface, where the spring effect is the strongest. An impact location more than half an inch away from the sweet spot can cause noticeable distance loss. In general, missing on the toe side loses less distance than on the heel side as the toe is farther away from the hands and thus has a slightly higher linear speed.

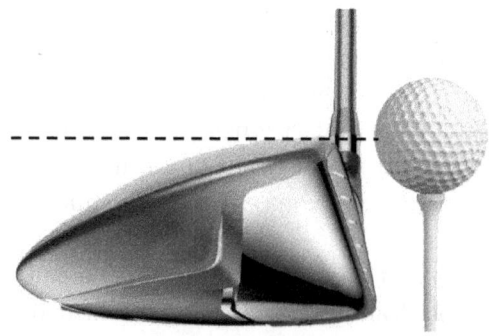

Fig. 8-7 Typical Tee Height for a Driver

Although a golfer can attack the ball at any angle with a driver, launch monitor data have revealed that striking a ball on the upswing arc, i.e., at a positive attack angle, can boosts carry distance.

Golfers are recommended to tee a ball up so that its top half is above the crown of the driver (Fig. 8-7). This setup facilitates ball striking on the upswing arc and makes it easier to hit the ball on the sweet spot of the clubface, or slightly above.

An impact location slightly above the sweet spot can result in a lower spin rate and a higher launch angle, a combination that is known to boost driving distance.

SMASH FACTOR

Smash factor is used to measure the relative impact quality of a shot. It is defined as the ratio of the ball speed right after impact to the clubhead speed right before impact.

Smash Factor = Ball Speed / Club Speed

For example, with a clubhead speed of 105 mph right before impact and a ball speed of 153 mph right after, the smash factor is:

Smash Factor = 153 / 105 = 1.46

The typical smash factor won't be the same for all clubs. As the club loft increases, the maximum smash factor achievable actually decreases because launch vector VL gets weaker, and that means a smaller portion of the clubhead kinetic energy is used to launch the ball. For instance, the smash factor can reach 1.5 in a drive but only 1.25 in a pitching wedge shot. Among PGA tour players, the average smash factor is 1.49 for the driver but drops to 1.38 for the 6-iron. In contrast, the average smash factor for drivers is about 1.45 among amateurs. Therefore, smash factor should only be used to compare shots from similar clubs. For a particular club, a higher smash factor indicates higher energy transfer efficiency and usually means the impact location is closer to the sweet spot.

CHECKING IMPACT LOCATIONS REGULARLY

Knowing the importance of making solid contact, golfers should be mindful of impact locations during practice and monitor them regularly. Many inexpensive off-the-shelf products can be used to mark impact locations. Powder spray, impact tapes, and dry erase markers are excellent products for this purpose.

Impact Tape

Impact tapes are self-adhesive stickers that change color upon impact. They are very effective in marking impact locations. The wonderful thing about impact tapes is that they can be used in both dry and wet environments. The downside is that they are more expensive than other solutions, and need to be replaced after a few shots. Besides, impact tapes may slightly alter the clubface properties, such as the friction coefficient and the coefficient of restitution (COR), and may affect ball speed and spin rate to some degree.

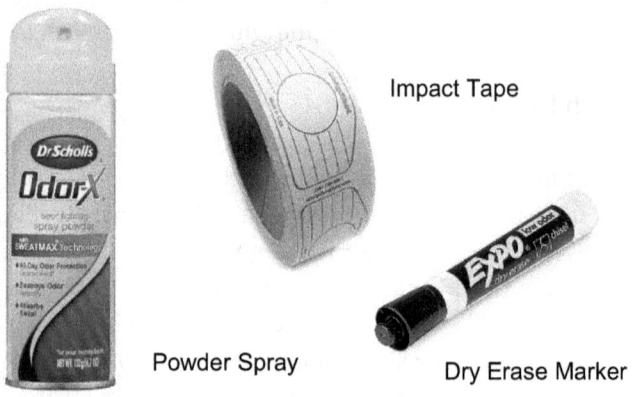

Fig. 8-8 Impact Marking Solutions

Powder Spray

Powder spray is another great product for marking impact locations. It is inexpensive, easy to apply, and can cover the entire clubface easily. Due to its ability to cover irregular surfaces, powder spray is perfect for marking shots hit on or near the hosel.

Unlike impact tapes, powder spray essentially keeps clubface properties intact. It is perfect for shots hit on a tee or from a mat. However, powder spray does not work very well in a wet environment or for ground shots because water, dirt, or grass juice tends to wipe off the powder either before or after impact.

There are powder spray products made specifically for golf. Yet some foot powder spray sold at retail stores works just as well and costs less. Dr. Scholl's Odor-X spray powder is a proven product for golf impact marking. The thin layer of white powder left on the clubface can be easily wiped off from irons, but over time might leave some residue on a clubface with black coating. Make sure to wash the clubface clean after a practice session.

Dry Erase Markers

Dry erase markers are also a good solution for impact marking. They are effective, inexpensive, and convenient to carry. Just like the powder spray, the dry erase ink barely affects the clubface properties.

To mark impact location, draw a big dot about a quarter inch in diameter on a golf ball using a dry erase marker and then place the ball down with the dot facing the club. During impact, the ink will be transferred to the clubface to mark the impact location. Rest assured, these marks can be easily wiped off with a wet towel afterward.

What is the downside of these markers? It does take some extra effort to draw a dot on each ball, and the put it down properly. Besides, dark marks may have poor visibility on a black clubface, which is quite common these days.

9. OFF-CENTER IMPACT

In the game of golf, the importance of making solid contact can never be overemphasized. Yet even great ball strikers will miss the sweet spot every now and then, especially when playing under pressure. After a hosel shot in 1971, former PGA tour player and TV commentator Johnny Miller revealed that for years his only swing thought was "Don't shank it!" Understanding what happens in an off-center shot will help golfers properly diagnose ball flight issues and find the right solutions.

OFF-CENTER SHOTS

There are mainly three types of off-center shots in golf: thin shots, heel shots, and toe shots. Thin shots, where the impact point is well below the sweet spot of the clubface, are very common among average golfers. In an extreme thin shot, a ball could be struck by the leading edge of the clubface. Heel and toe shots are self-explanatory. The extreme case of a heel shot is also known as a shank, where the ball makes contact with the hosel. For drivers, it is also possible to catch the ball too high on the clubface. In a really bad shot, the ball could make a dent on the crown and shoot up like a rocket.

First, we are going to demonstrate the effects of impact location using a simple experiment. We will need an old putter and a small hammer. A fairway wood or a hybrid can substitute for the putter and a golf ball may replace the hammer. If so desired, put some masking tape on the clubface for protection.

Hold the putter's grip end gently between the thumb and index finger, making sure the club can swing freely. With the putter at rest, tap the center of the clubface using the hammer or golf ball, as illustrated in Fig. 9-1. You will notice that the whole putter head moves straight back, and the fingers holding the grip barely feel any shock. In addition, the sound of impact is solid, crispy, and pleasant to hear. This is a solid strike because the force from the hammer points at the CG of the putter and produces no torque.

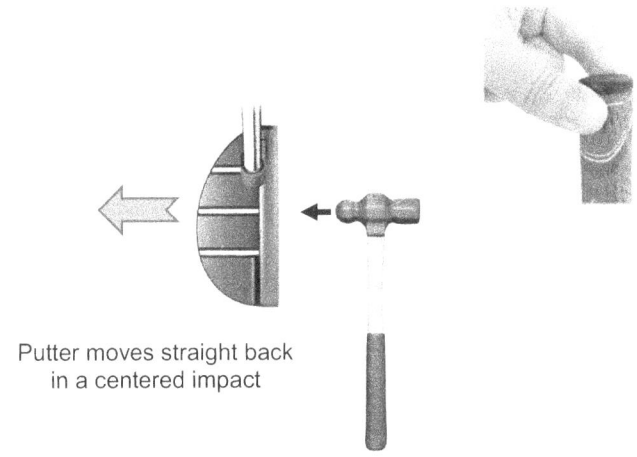

Fig. 9-1 Centered Impact

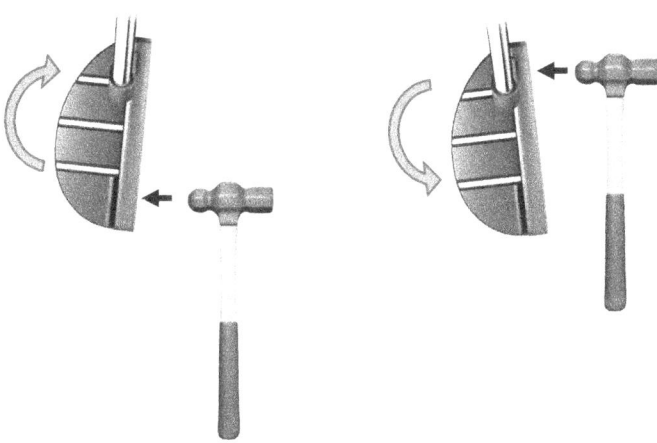

Fig. 9-2 Off-center Impacts

Wait for the putter to come to a complete stop, and then gently tap on its toe or heel side, as shown in Fig. 9-2. This time the putter head will twist vigorously and the sound of impact is hollow and dull. The fingers holding the putter will feel a shock. The putter head will still move back, but only for a shorter distance, because a good part of the energy has been used to drive the rotation.

The clubhead twisting is the result of impact torque, which is the product of impact force and the distance between the impact point and the sweet spot. Since the impact torque in an off-center strike is not zero, it will cause the clubhead to rotate around the CG.

The clubface rotates counterclockwise around its CG in a heel strike and becomes closed, whereas in a toe shot it rotates clockwise and becomes open. The change of clubface orientation inevitably changes a ball's launch direction and spin. At higher speeds, the clubhead twisting in an off-center shot is quite severe since the torque is very strong.

MOMENT OF INERTIA (MOI)

Various clubs may respond to the same off-center impact differently, depending on the weight distribution of the clubhead. For example, with the same impact torque, a cavity-back iron tends to be more resistant to twisting than a blade type and won't alter the launch direction as much. In other words, cavity-back irons are more forgiving.

A club's ability to resist angular (i.e., rotational) acceleration is measured by an attribute called *moment of inertia* (MOI). Under the same impact torque, an object with a higher MOI will have less twisting or rotation. For example, a figure skater would spin slower when she extends her arms because that move increases her MOI. Likewise, we can increase a clubhead's MOI by putting more weight towards the perimeter.

A cavity-back iron has more weight distributed along the perimeter (i.e. perimeter weighting technology) and typically has a greater MOI than a blade iron. For off-center shots, a cavity-back iron tends to deliver better results than a blade. Most game-improvement irons use cavity-back design and they make ball striking much easier for average golfers. However, blade irons offer better distance and feel for solid shots. Imagine hitting a nail with a hammer as opposed to using a skillet and you will get the idea.

GEAR EFFECT FOR WOODS

A driver's CG can be more than an inch behind the clubface, depending on the head size and weight distribution (Fig. 9-3). The distance from its CG to the clubface presents an issue: it will amplify a small-angle rotation and turn it into a significant lateral movement. In Fig. 9-3, a spot on the clubface moves sideways for a noticeable distance when a driver rotates around its CG for a small angle.

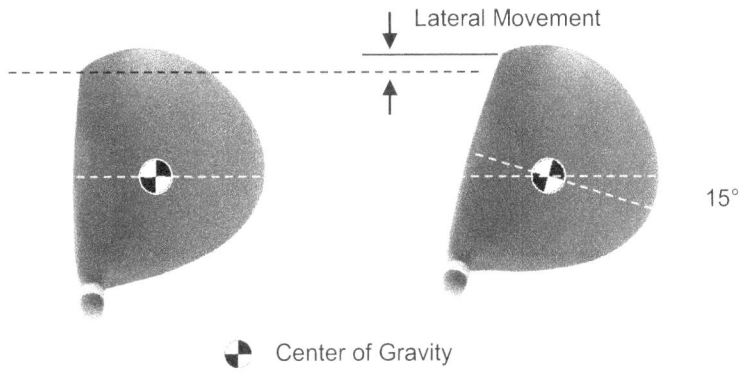

Fig. 9-3 CG of a Driver

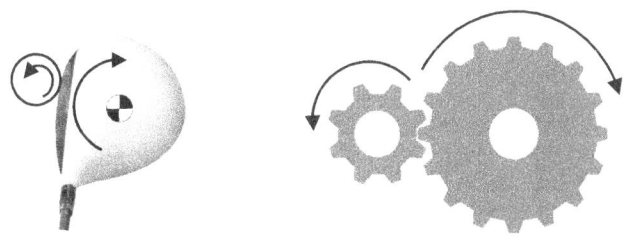

Fig. 9-4 Gear Action and Gear Effect

As the clubhead rotates during impact, surface friction causes the ball to roll on the clubface and creates sidespin, just like what would happen to a pair of engaged gears. This phenomenon is therefore called the gear effect (Fig. 9-4).

The gear effect on the horizontal plane will impart sidespin to a ball. A toe impact will produce counterclockwise sidespin and cause a ball to launch right and then curve left, i.e., a draw for right-handed golfers. Likewise, a heel impact will produce clockwise sidespin and cause a ball to launch left then curve right, i.e., a fade for right-handed golfers (Fig. 9-5).

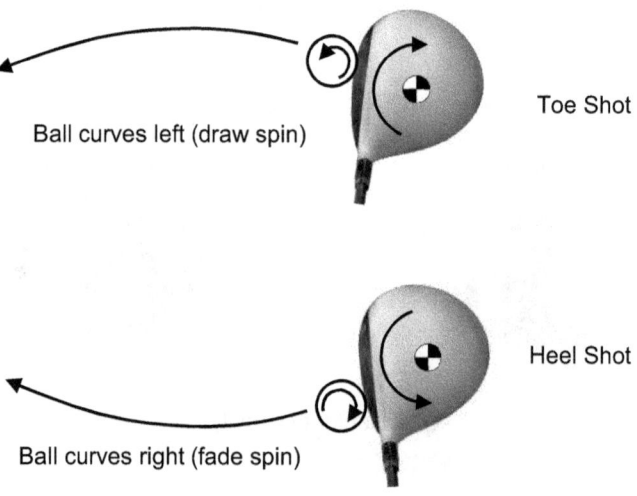

Fig. 9-5 Horizontal Gear Effect

Fig. 9-6 Vertical Gear Effect

Off-center Impact

Gear effect can also happen in the vertical direction. An impact below the sweet spot will enhance backspin, whereas one above the sweet spot will impart topspin, which will partially cancel out the backspin produced by the club loft, resulting in reduced final backspin (Fig. 9-6).

GEAR EFFECT FOR IRONS

Gear effect is the result of the clubface's lateral movement, which is related to the distance between the clubface and the clubhead CG. Therefore, things are quite different for an iron, whose CG is much closer to the clubface than in a driver (Fig. 9-7).

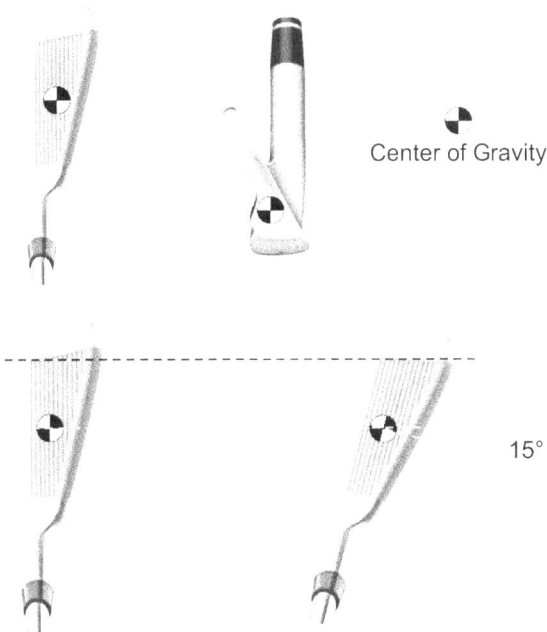

Fig. 9-7 CG of an Iron

When an iron rotates around its CG on a horizontal plane for the same angle, a spot on its clubface mainly moves back and forth in the target line direction (Fig. 9-7). The lateral movement is trivial compared to that of a driver and the gear effect is negligible.

BULGE

You probably have wondered why the clubface of a driver is not flat. The bulge, which is the curvature from heel to toe, usually tracks the arc of a circle. For example, the bulge shown in Fig. 9-8 has a radius of ten inches.

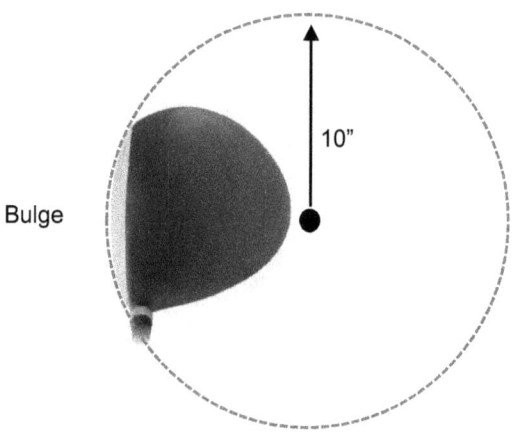

Fig. 9-8 Bulge

    The bulge isn't put in place to make a driver look more fashionable; it is there for a practical purpose: to offset the gear effect so a driver can be more forgiving to off-center shots.

    On the toe side, the clubface is open due to the bulge and will launch a toe shot slightly towards the right side with CW (clockwise) sidespin, just like what happens in a solid open-face iron shot. This CW sidespin goes against the CCW (counterclockwise) sidespin induced by the gear effect in a toe shot. If the two types of sidespin completely cancel out each other, the ball will launch straight as a push shot. Ideally, we want to have a bulge design that allows the CW sidespin to partially offset the gear effect CCW sidespin. With the right amount of CCW sidespin left, the ball will be able to launch right and then draw back near the target line.

    Likewise, for a heel shot the bulge presents a closed clubface and will impart CCW sidespin to offset the CW sidespin caused by the gear effect, ideally allowing the ball to launch left and then fade back near the target line.

In order to properly offset the horizontal gear effect so an off-center shot can land near the target line, the bulge curvature has to be carefully designed. The ideal radius of the bulge depends on multiple factors, which include impact location, swing speed, and the MOI of the driver, etc. *It is evident that one bulge design won't provide perfect compensation for all off-center shots.* A driver design is most likely optimized only for the high-probability off-center shots, such as those missing the sweet spot by an inch or less. For moderate off-center shots, a well-designed driver may do a decent job.

However, don't expect miracles if you miss the sweet spot by two inches. According to TaylorMade, the traditional bulge and roll design doesn't always work as expected for extreme off-center shots. For example, a high toe shot tends to land to the left of the target line and spin significantly less, whereas a low heel shot tends to land to the right of the target line with much higher spin.

ROLL

The clubface of a driver also has a subtle curvature from crown to sole, which is referred to as the roll (Fig. 9-9). This feature is put in place to offset the vertical gear effect.

Fig. 9-9 Roll

For an off-center shot hit above the sweet spot, the backspin rate could be too low to maximize the carry distance. By implementing the curvature along the vertical direction, the upper part of the clubface will launch a ball at a higher angle to get more distance. Likewise, the lower part of the clubface will launch a ball with a higher backspin rate but at a lower angle so the ball won't rise too high in the air and lose distance.

DEALING WITH GEAR EFFECTS

Keep in mind that the bulge is designed based on the assumption that a driver would deliver a square-strike at the sweet spot. For a swing that would nonetheless produce a big slice even if the ball was caught on the sweet spot, we probably shouldn't be surprised if an off-center shot doesn't come back to the fairway. In other words, the bulge won't fix a swing plane or swing path problem.

Ball flight can get really complicated at times, it is important that golfers be aware of the gear effect and be mindful of it during practice. When diagnosing bad shots, it is always a good idea to first check impact locations before drawing any conclusion and making swing adjustments.

GEAR EFFECT EXAMPLES

The following examples demonstrate how gear effect can lead to misinterpretation of ball flight and how important it is to monitor impact locations.

Example 1: Horizontal Gear Effect

In an actual shot, the ball launched slightly right and then hooked back to the left, as shown in Fig. 9-10. Had the ball been hit on the sweet spot of the driver, the clubface must have pointed slightly right and moved drastically from inside to outside. Yet the data captured by the launch monitor didn't agree with the speculation.

Launch monitor data revealed that the golfer was only swinging slightly from inside to outside (1.0° to the right) and the

Off-center Impact

center of the clubface was pointing to the target. Had he caught the ball on the sweet spot of the clubface, this would have produced a nearly straight shot, or at most a very subtle draw,

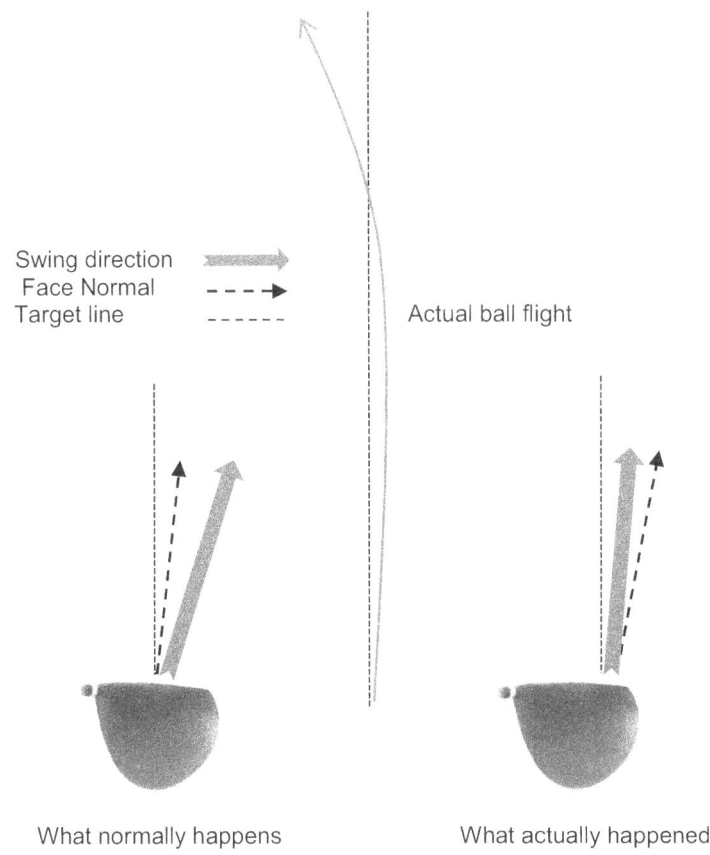

Fig. 9-10 Horizontal Gear Effect

It turned out the golfer had struck the ball on the toe side of the clubface. With the center of the clubface square to the target line, the impact location at the toe pointed slightly right due to the bulge. Obviously, gear effect kicked in and imparted to the ball strong counterclockwise sidespin. In this particular case, it appeared that the bulge didn't offer the right amount of compensation for this impact location, and the ball landed to the left of the target line. This is the exact issue observed by Taylormade in its research.

The golfer planned a straight shot but hit a hook instead because of a toe side impact. This case underscores the importance of making solid contact and checking impact locations during ball flight analyses.

Example 2: Horizontal Gear Effect

At the 2013 Hyundai Tournament of Champions, Dustin Johnson hit a snap hook (i.e. a severe hook) off the tee. The high-speed swing video showed that the clubface twisted open drastically at impact. Many people found that hard to explain: how could you hit a snap hook with the clubface wide open?

In fact, that was a typical case of horizontal gear effect caught on camera. The clubface twisted open because the ball collided with the toe of the driver, and the gear effect put CCW hook spin on the ball.

Two factors had contributed to the hook. First, the ball was caught on far side of the toe, as evidenced by the vigorous clubhead twisting. As we have mentioned before, the driver design is only optimized for certain moderate off-center shots. TaylorMade has confirmed that the traditional driver design doesn't perform well for those extreme cases. Second, Dustin Johnson had very high clubhead speeds. That means the torque produced in that toe shot was huge, and the gear effect was so strong that it exceeded what the clubhead could compensate.

Example 3: Vertical Gear Effect

A high backspin rate, when combined with a very high ball speed, can cause a ball to rise too high during its flight and lose carry distance as well as rolling power. This is undesirable unless a golfer plans to hit the green and wants the ball to stick upon landing.

A good drive typically has a spin rate of 2000~3000 rpm. The average drive spin rate is 2686 rpm for the PGA Tour and 2611 for LPGA players according to the data provided by Trackman.

In an actual drive, a ball was launched at a very low angle but with an unusually high spin rate of 4300 rpm. The ball carried only

245 yards, quite disappointing for a clubhead speed of 112 mph. Visual inspection confirmed that the ball was struck on the lower part of the clubface and this was a typical example of vertical gear effect.

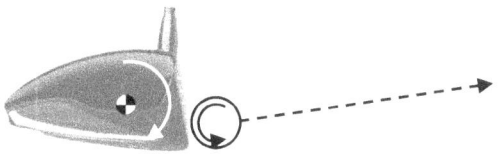

Bottom impact: lower launch angle, higher spin rate

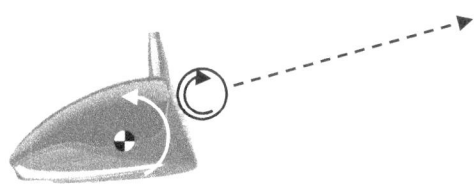

Top impact: higher launch angle, lower spin rate

Fig. 9-11 Vertical Gear Effect

In the next drive, the ball was put on a higher tee and struck on the upper part of the clubface. The launch angle increased to 11°, and the spin rate dropped to 3100 rpm. With the same clubhead speed, the carry distance jumped to 275 yards!

10. Golf Balls

The discussion of ball flight won't be complete without talking about balls. Golf balls may look alike, but they don't necessarily behave the same. The dimple design, internal structure, and material for each layer ultimately affect a ball's launch condition and aerodynamic performance. Knowing the basics of golf balls will help golfers better understand ball flight and choose the right balls for their games.

Golf Ball Specifications

Golfers can use any balls in recreational rounds, but that is not the case in regulated competitions. In the USA, the requirements concerning golf balls are governed by the USGA (United States Golf Association), which maintains the specifications and a list of approved golf balls.

Overall, there are three major physical requirements that a golf ball must meet in order to be approved by the USGA: weight, size, and symmetry. A ball's initial velocity and overall distance are also restricted so the existing golf courses don't become outdated too quickly as technologies advance.

Weight

The weight of a regulated golf ball shall not exceed 1.620 ounces or 45.93 grams. However, the USGA stipulates no minimum weight for golf balls. In theory, manufacturers could make golf balls as light as a feather if they wish.

Golf Balls

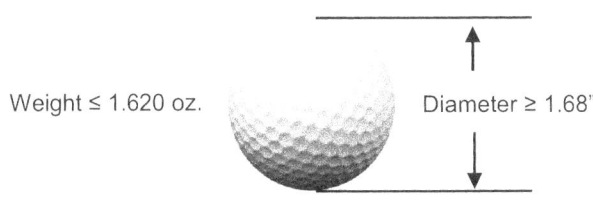

Fig. 10-1 Weight and Size of a Golf Ball

Size

The diameter of a regulated golf ball must be at least 1.680 inches, or 42.67mm (Fig. 10-1). Surprisingly, there is no upper limit to a ball's size. A golf ball could be as big as a basketball and would still conform to the rules. In 2019, Callaway released SuperSoft Magna, an oversized golf ball that is 1.73 inches in diameter. With a slightly higher CG, it is supposed to make ball striking a little easier for beginners.

In the past, golfers playing under the R&A rules in the UK had the option of using a smaller ball, which was 1.62 inches in diameter. The smaller ball, referred to as the "British ball" by Americans, could be used in the British Open but was illegal in the United States. The difference between a "British ball" and an "American ball" in diameter was only 0.06 inch, the thickness of a penny. The R&A banned the smaller balls in British Open starting in 1974 but didn't fully adopt the rules used by the USGA until 1990.

Symmetry

Besides the requirements on weight and size, a golf ball must also have symmetrical physical properties. The intention is to ensure that a ball has symmetrical aerodynamic performance. Why is this important at all? As will be explained later, asymmetrical dimple designs can be used to manipulate a ball's behavior in the air to give players certain advantage.

Ball Construction

The USGA rules require a player to use the same type of ball during the play of a hole. In professional events, players may be required to use golf balls of the same brand, same model, and even the same color for the entire game.

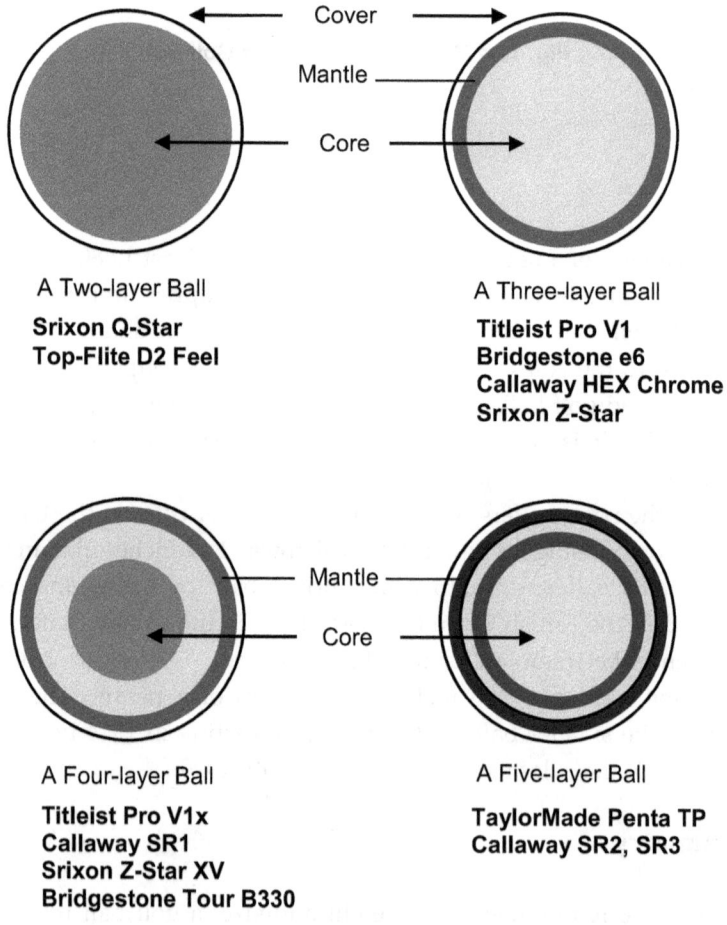

A Two-layer Ball
Srixon Q-Star
Top-Flite D2 Feel

A Three-layer Ball
Titleist Pro V1
Bridgestone e6
Callaway HEX Chrome
Srixon Z-Star

A Four-layer Ball
Titleist Pro V1x
Callaway SR1
Srixon Z-Star XV
Bridgestone Tour B330

A Five-layer Ball
TaylorMade Penta TP
Callaway SR2, SR3

Fig. 10-2 Ball Constructions

Therefore, ball manufacturers strive to provide balanced golf balls that have good performance for all clubs: drivers, fairway woods, irons, and putters.

A modern golf ball is typically made of two or more layers to achieve balanced performance. A multilayer ball is built using different materials for each layer, which usually also has a different thickness (Fig. 10-2).

In general, the carry distance is closely related to the core material, whereas spin and feel are determined by both the cover and the core. For shots around the green, the cover has more influence on spin and feel than the core, which is not fully compressed in such shots. In a drive, the core is significantly compressed and therefore also affects spin and feel.

Two-layer Balls

Two-layer balls are the most popular among recreational golfers. They are easier to make, less expensive, and longer-lasting. A two-layer ball typically uses hard and durable cover materials. These balls tend to travel longer distances and have a lower spin rate than premium balls. They are great for drives but do not have the best performance around the green because they cannot stop quickly upon landing due to the low spin. Most range balls and low-cost golf balls are manufactured using the two-layer construction.

Multilayer Balls

Most premium balls use a three-layer construction, but some can have four or more layers. For example, a Titleist Pro V1 has three layers, but a Pro V1x has four. We also start seeing more balls made of four or more layers. A TaylorMade Penta TP has five layers while a Maxfli U/6 has as many as six layers.

Premium balls use softer and more expensive cover materials to boost spin for approach shots. When working in tandem with a high-performance wedge, these balls can acquire superior spin rates even from the rough. They are designed to achieve a balanced performance for both long and approach shots and are more suitable for skilled players. Average golfers might not compress these balls enough to get the low spin needed in drives.

COVER MATERIALS

The material and thickness of the cover layer will affect a ball's spin, speed, and feel. Cover stiffness affects ball spin more. Soft cover materials can boost greenside spin but also tend to reduce ball speed in long shots.

Cover thickness has more influence on speed than on spin. Since the cover material usually has a lower coefficient of restitution (COR) than the core, a golf ball with a thicker cover layer tends to have a weaker "spring effect" and consequently a lower speed.

The two most popular cover materials in use today are Surlyn and urethane.

Surlyn

Surlyn is a family of ionomer resins produced by DuPont. The majority of the two-layer golf balls on the market use Surlyn as their cover material. These balls tend to have lower drive spin and hence fly straighter off the tee.

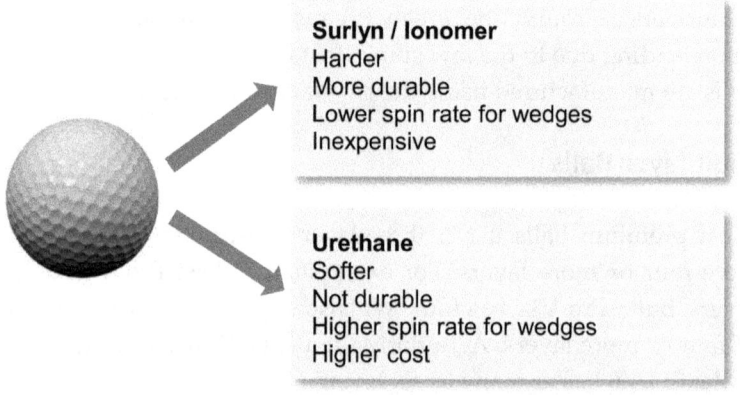

Fig. 10-3 Golf Ball Cover Materials

Urethane

Urethane is a type of synthetic material, which is softer but more expensive than Surlyn. It is usually used on premium balls, such as Titleist Pro V1/V1x, Bridgestone Tour B330, and Srixon Z-star, etc.

Balls covered with urethane feel softer and have higher spin for shots near the green. If a ball hits the green and stops abruptly or even rolls backward, we can almost be sure it is covered with urethane or other soft materials.

DIMPLES

Dimples are the small indentations on a golf ball. They are not there to make a ball pretty, but to serve aerodynamic purposes. Dimples can reduce air resistance. More importantly, they help produce the gravity-fighting Magnus force. In general, dimples allow a golf ball to stay in the air longer and travel farther.

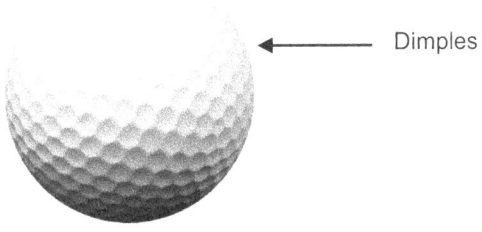

Fig. 10-4 Dimples

The quantity and shape of the dimples affect a ball's spin rate, trajectory, and travel distance. Ball manufacturers have plenty of freedom in dimple design since the USGA doesn't care how many dimples are put on a golf ball or the shape they take.

Golf balls from different brands or models often have different dimple designs. The number of dimples also varies. For example, a Titleist Pro V1 produced in 2018 has 352 dimples, whereas a Pro V1x has only 328. A Bridgestone B330 golf ball, as its name suggests, has 330 dimples that look much different than the ones on a Pro V1.

However, the USGA does care about one thing: dimple design and distribution must be symmetrical so a ball has uniform aerodynamic performance. Balls that don't meet this requirement won't be authorized for regulated tournaments. It is worth mentioning that this symmetry requirement has a shockingly high price tag of 1.375 million dollars, as explained below.

Anti-slice Golf Balls

In the late 1970s, a company named Polara produced a special type of golf ball, which featured asymmetrical dimple design and layout. The dimples around the spin equator were shallower, whereas those near the poles were deeper. Polara claimed these balls had self-correcting and anti-slice capabilities.

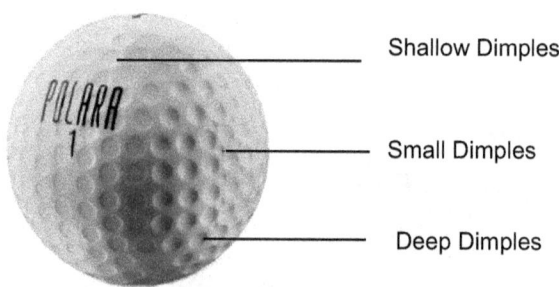

Fig. 10-5 Polara Self-correcting Golf Ball

When set up properly, the asymmetrical dimple design induces extra air resistance to attenuate the sidespin and forces the ball to fly straighter. A mishit shot would therefore travel with reduced curvature, which can be as much as 75% less than that from a regular ball. To get the advertised benefits, a Polara ball must be put down with a specific orientation, which is only possible for tee shots. These balls suffer from reduced lift in the air and don't travel as far as regular balls.

It turned out that the USGA wasn't happy about these balls and refused to sanction them for tournament use. In 1978, Polara sued the USGA, claiming its business was damaged by the decision. In 1981, the USGA changed the Rule of Golf by adding the symmetry requirement on golf balls and eventually settled the lawsuit in 1985 for 1.375 million dollars.

COMPRESSION

The compression rating measures how difficult it is to compress a golf ball using a static load and represents how hard a ball feels at impact. Unlike size and weight, compression is not currently regulated by the USGA, and no standardized test has been established. One of the test methods applies 200-pound load on a ball and subtracts one point for every 0.001" of deformation from a baseline number of 180.

Compression = 180 - (deformation/0.001)

With this formula, it is possible to have a negative compression rating. For example, 0.200" in deformation corresponds to a compression rating of -20. Typical compression ratings are between 40 and 120. A ball with a higher compression rating feels harder at impact. Balls rated below 70 are considered soft, whereas those rated over 90 are deemed hard.

Compression rating is mainly determined by the core. A ball with a lower compression rating usually has a lower spin rate in drives and fairway wood shots, as a drastically compressed ball on a low-loft clubface doesn't roll very well to produce the entitled spin rate. Actually, low spin is desirable in long tee shots since it usually boosts distance, and also reduces the chance of hitting slice or hook.

Yet the core has limited influence on spin performance for shots around the green because it doesn't deform much in such low-speed and high-loft shots. Ball spin in shots around the green is mainly determined by the cover material.

Both low and high compression balls have similar performance in carry distance. Players with high swing speeds can play low compression balls and won't lose distance. However, golfers with low swing speeds may get too much spin playing high compression balls because they don't compress the ball enough.

Another benefit of low compression balls is that they perform well in both hot and cold environments, whereas high compression balls tend to lose distance in very cold days.

According to Wilson Sporting Goods, the majority of the golfers surveyed prefer softer balls regardless of their skill levels. Since a lower compression golf ball deforms easier and feels softer, golfers tend to feel more confident and more relaxed, and ultimately swing better using these balls. Nobody likes the feeling of hitting a rock! This may also explain why low compression soft balls are becoming more popular. The Wilson DX2 Soft ball boasts a compression rating of 29 and is advertised as the softest golf ball on the market!

CHOOSING THE RIGHT BALLS

Tour players and low handicap golfers usually know what type of balls suits their games. For them, the urethane-covered premium balls offer balanced performance for both drives and approach shots.

For average golfers who are not capable of landing their approach shots on the green very often, spin performance around the green doesn't matter as much. Keeping the ball in the fairway is far more important to them. It is better for them to choose low compression soft balls that offer lower spin and longer distance off the tee.

11. Grooves and Spin

Grooves Matter?

In the 1960s, a British research team led by Alastair Cochran and John Strobbs conducted some interesting experiments to study how grooves affected golf shots. Their findings, which were published in a book titled *Search for the Perfect Swing* in 1968, were quite counterintuitive and shocking to many people.

The team tested three sets of clubs: 5-irons, 7-irons, and 9-irons in the experiments. Each set consisted of two clubs: one with grooves and one without. The two clubs in each set were otherwise identical.

They concluded that there was no distinguishable difference between the two faces when hitting balls from *dry and clean* lies. With the grooved clubs, the backspin rates were slightly higher, and the carry and total distances were slightly shorter. For example, the backspin rate was 7380 rpm for the grooved 7-iron and 7260 rpm for the smooth-face counterpart; and the average carry distances were 137 and 138 yards respectively. In other words, the grooves didn't make much difference for dry and clean shots.

They also concluded that there was no performance difference between the two clubs in each set when the clubfaces were sprayed with clean water. Their book didn't mention any test from the rough, where grass could be caught between the ball and the clubface. This is a very important scenario to consider since grass juice is a very effective lubricant, which can reduce ball spin.

The findings can be puzzling to many golfers considering the heated discussions on grooves these days. Due to this book's status in the golf industry, a lot of people are still quoting it today to question the importance of grooves.

Do grooves really matter?

Actually, their conclusions do make some sense, because the tremendous pressure at impact can create enough friction for a ball to stop sliding in time, even on a smooth-face club, provided the club has a low or medium loft angle, such as the 5-irons and 7-irons tested. However, the buzz on grooves nowadays is mainly associated with high-loft wedges, the scoring clubs in the game. Interesting enough, the British team didn't mention any wedge testing, nor did they provide spin data for the 9-irons.

The fact is, golf ball spin is a very complicated subject and involves numerous factors, including ball material, ball construction, groove geometry, interfacial material, club loft, impact location, and swing speed, etc. While the findings of the British team may be true and valid, the scope of their experiments was very limited, and the conclusions should not be generalized or extended to all scenarios.

THE GROOVE CONTROVERSY

Groove design has gone through different stages in the evolution of iron clubs. The V and U grooves, which were named according to their cross-sectional shapes, are the two most important ones in history (Fig. 11-1). The V grooves were mostly used on irons made before 1981 and were put on the clubfaces by stamping. It is reasonable to assume that the British research team used irons with V grooves in their experiments.

In order to improve club manufacturability, the USGA changed the rules in 1981 to allow U grooves. In 1984, Karsten Manufacturing Corporation (now PING) incorporated the U grooves on its PING Eye2 irons and became the first company to take advantage of the new rules. In case you didn't know, Karsten's founder, Karsten Solheim, was the inventor of the renowned PING Anser putter and the pioneer of the perimeter weighting technology, which is being widely used in today's cavity-back game improvement irons.

Thanks to the U grooves, the PING Eye2 irons demonstrated much better spin performance from the rough than competing products, which were still using the V grooves. However, the edges of these original U grooves were so sharp that they would leave terrible groove marks on a ball's cover and quickly rendered it unfit for play. At some point, these U grooves became known as the "square grooves" although their cross-sectional shape was never a square.

To solve the ball-chewing problem, Karsten modified the U grooves in 1985 by rounding the edges with a tiny radius, which made the groove width on the clubface slightly exceed the USGA specification at the time, although the distance from wall to wall still met the requirement. Because the difference was so trivial (about the thickness of a personal check), Karsten didn't think it was necessary to resubmit the modified design to the USGA for approval.

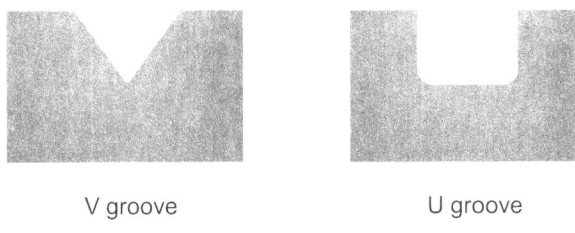

V groove   U groove

Fig. 11-1 V and U Grooves

With the U grooves, rough became less challenging for tour players, and driving accuracy was no longer the key ingredient in the winning equation. Players using the U-groove irons could hit from the rough and still produce a decent amount of spin to stop the balls on the green. The "Bomb and Gouge" playing style, which focused on maximizing driving distance instead of landing the ball in the fairway, became popular on the PGA tour.

Before long, a group of tour players complained that the stronger backspin from Eye2 irons gave their players an unfair advantage. The PGA Tour, after testing the Eye2 irons, concluded that these irons indeed produced higher backspin rates than irons with V grooves, especially for shots hit from the rough. The USGA also evaluated the Eye2 irons and claimed that the grooves were nonconforming.

Here came the problem. The USGA didn't specify how the groove width should be measured at that time. Karsten measured the groove width from wall to wall and argued that they met the requirement. The USGA, on the other hand, claimed the groove width on the surface should also meet the specification. Even though the Eye2 irons' grooves were slightly wider on the clubface, the difference was comparable to the diameter of a human hair.

In 1989, Karsten sued the USGA and PGA Tour for 100 million dollars each, claiming his business had been negatively affected by the groove controversy. Both cases were later settled out of court with the USGA and PGA Tour grandfathering the Eye2 irons manufactured between 1985 and 1989.

THE USGA'S GROOVE STUDY

As the trend of "Bomb and Gouge" gradually getting out of control and taking the game of golf to a different direction, the USGA felt the need to do something "to protect the fundamental challenges of the game and ensure that skill, not an overreliance on technology, is the prime determinant of success in the game."

In 2005, the USGA and the R&A jointly started a project, which took a couple of years to complete, to study how groove geometry affected the spin rate. The project team conducted numerous tests on more than 100 different groove configurations in the lab. It also verified lab results on real turf using tour players and amateur golfers. In 2006 and 2007, the USGA published its findings in two reports, which are well worth reading for golfers who want to know more about the effects of grooves.

The USGA's research reveals that grooves indeed play a crucial role in ball spin, which is a key element in golf ball flight, especially for shots hit from the rough. Their conclusions may seem to contradict those drawn by the British researchers, who claimed that grooves didn't affect ball spin or distance. Since ball spin is such a complex subject that involves a number of variables, it is fair to say that the British team was only looking at the issue from a very limited view and its conclusions are not universally applicable.

In a nutshell, the USGA's research reveals that ball spin rate can be affected by groove design, club loft, lie conditions, ball properties, and even the swing quality (Fig. 11-2).

Certain grooves can produce higher spin rates when they are

used with a particular type of balls, but won't necessarily have the same effect with another type. Some grooves produce similar spin rates regardless of the balls used.

Case in point, a wedge with U grooves can produce decent spin rate from the rough when urethane-covered premium balls are used, but won't be able to achieve the same result with Surlyn-covered balls. In contrast, a wedge with V grooves will experience drastic spin reduction from the rough no matter what type of ball is used.

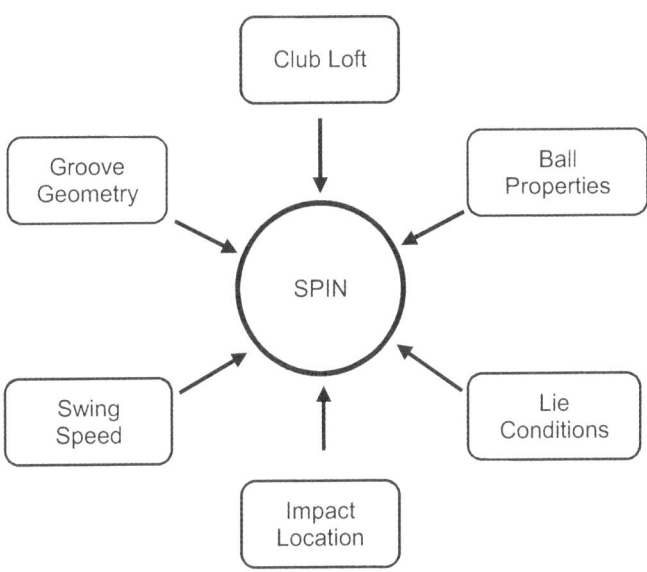

Fig. 11-2 Spin Factors

THE USGA'S KEY FINDINGS ON GROOVES

The USGA's research confirms that modern groove design and face treatment provide significant performance enhancement in terms of spin generation over the traditional V grooves. Here is a summary of the key findings from the study:

1. For dry and clean impacts, the spin rates from U grooves and V grooves are indistinguishable (Report 1, p28).
2. With wet interfacial materials, the U grooves show significant performance improvement over the V grooves in producing spin (Report 1, p31). Both grooves outperform the clubs with no grooves (Report 2, p14).
3. For U grooves, a smaller edge radius (0.005") produced greater spin than a larger radius (0.010"). Edge radius doesn't affect spin rate with the V grooves (Report 2, p15)
4. Width, depth, and spacing of the grooves also affect the spin rate. In general, with an edge radius of 0.010" or greater, increasing the cross-sectional area of the grooves per linear inch increases the spin rate (Report 2, P18). That means increasing the groove depth or/and width will boost spin; decreasing the groove pitch also increases spin.
5. Milling (roughening the surface area of the club) within the conforming 180-microinch limit has no appreciable effect on spin (Report 2, p25).
6. With the same groove design, the spin rate increases with the loft angle in dry conditions, but this is not necessarily true in wet conditions (Report 1, p15). For example, the spin rate of a sand wedge is greater than that of an 8-iron in a dry impact. But in wet conditions, an 8-iron produces higher spin than a sand wedge.
7. The shape and edge radius of the grooves affect the spin of the urethane-covered balls, but have little influence on that of the Surlyn-covered ones (Report 2, p32, p52). In other words, playing the premium balls using an iron with V grooves or worn-out U grooves doesn't deliver the best results. On the other hand, if you play Surlyn-covered balls, then U grooves won't give you much advantage either.

Now we can better understand Cochran and Strobbs' research findings. Their claim that grooves have no influence on ball spin is only true under certain conditions. The statement is not necessarily valid for other loft angles, lie conditions, or ball types.

THE NEW GROOVE RULES

In 2008, the USGA and R&A, based on their findings in the groove research project, proposed an addition to the Rules of Golf to restrict groove volume and edge radius. The key requirements of the addition, known as the Condition of Competition, are as follows:

- Grooves must have a symmetrical cross-section.
- Groove width must not exceed 0.035" and groove depth must not exceed 0.020".
- The cross-sectional area of a groove divided by the pitch will be limited to 0.0030 square inch per inch (0.0762 mm²/mm), except for drivers.
- For clubs with a loft of 25° or above, groove edge sharpness shall be in the form of a round having an effective minimum radius between 0.010 and 0.020 inches.

Apparently, the new rules don't ban the use of square grooves (i.e., U grooves) as many people had mistakenly claimed. The rules only put restrictions on the groove dimensions to limit the spin rate in shots hit from the rough. The main purpose is to bring back challenges to the game and to reward players with better shot-making skills.

The new groove rules took effect on January 1, 2010 for PGA tour events and major championships, such as U.S. Open. Starting in 2011, all clubs must be manufactured with grooves conforming to the new rules.

In 2010, a group conducted extensive tests to evaluate how the groove changes had affected the wedge performance. The tests compared brand new 56° wedges with updated grooves against those with pre-2010 grooves. All tests used Titleist Pro V1 urethane-covered balls. Shots were hit by scratch golfers from both fairway and rough lies. The tests revealed that wedges with pre-2010 grooves produced 9% more spin from the fairway, and 48% more from the rough than the ones with updated grooves. Besides the reduced spin, the updated 2010 grooves also caused balls to roll farther on the green after landing.

Keep the Grooves Clean and Fresh

Grooves on a wedge will wear out significantly after extensive usage. The main symptom is dull upper edges for grooves in the impact area, as shown in Fig. 11-3.

Fig. 11-3 Worn-out Grooves on a Wedge

A worn-out wedge tends to produce less spin and launch a ball at a higher angle. The spin reduction can be significant even for dry fairways shots and will be much worse for shots hit from the rough.

In 2017, Titleist's wedge team conducted tests to evaluate how groove conditions affect a ball's launch, spin, and on-green performance. In the experiments, they used a swing robot to hit balls and a launch monitor to collect ball flight data. According to the published video, the balls were hit from a mat. They compared brand new wedges with ones that have been used for 125 and 75 rounds respectively.

The results revealed that the condition of the grooves did affect the spin rate and launch angle, even from a dry and clean lie. Here is what they reported back: wedges with newer grooves will launch a ball at a slightly lower angle and with a higher spin rate. Upon landing on the green, the ball also has a shorter rolling distance, which is desirable for approach shots. The test results are listed in Table 11-1.

Table 11-1 Titleist Vokey Wedge Test Results

Wedge	Launch Angle	Spin (rpm)	Rolling (ft)
125-round	35°	6500	24
75-round	34°	7700	18
New	33°	8500	10

The difference is remarkable. The spin rates from the 75-round and 125-round wedges are 9.4% and 23.5% lower than that from a brand new wedge.

Titleist's test results were also validated by other individuals who tested wedges from different brands. For example, one golfer reported a launch angle of 33° and a spin rate of 10465 rpm from a brand new wedge, as opposed to a 35° launch angle and a spin rate of 7700 rpm from a used one. Another golfer reported 12000 rpm from a brand new 56° wedge, but got only 9000 rpm from a used one (same model). One PGA pro also made a YouTube video comparing a brand new 60° grooved wedge with a grooveless one. Hitting from a dry and clean mat, the grooved wedge produced a spin rate of 12000 rpm, whereas the grooveless one yielded only 6000 rpm. For actual chipping around the green, the grooved wedge also demonstrated much better spin performance.

GROOVES ON A DRIVER

A driver typically has a very small loft angle (8~12 degrees), which means the spinning vector is quite weak and doesn't require strong friction to get a ball into pure rolling. In addition, a driver is used to hit tee shots most of the time, so we don't need to worry about water, grass, or other debris getting between the ball and the clubface. Last but not the least, a very high spin rate is actually not desirable for a drive since it can cause the ball to rise too high in the air and thus lose carry distance and rolling power.

For these reasons, there is little benefit in putting grooves on a driver's clubface. As a matter of fact, deep grooves on the thin face of a driver may weaken its spring effect, as well as its structural integrity and durability. That is why most drivers don't even have any real grooves near their sweet spot. Some drivers may have a few shallow score lines in the center area, but those are mainly for decoration and visual reference purposes (Fig.11-4).

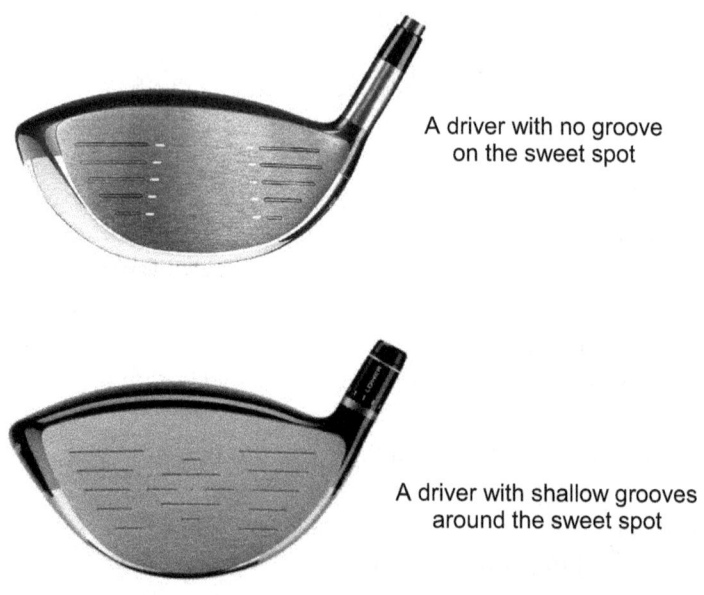

Fig. 11-4 Clubface of Drivers

In fact, recreational golfers have long been known to apply lubricating materials, such as butter, petroleum jelly, cooking spray etc., to the clubface of a driver to reduce backspin and sidespin so they can hit shots with increased accuracy. Bear in mind though, this trick, which is known as "greasing", is illegal in competition.

12. IRON SWING VS. DRIVER SWING

A smooth and good-looking swing may actually be problematic if it does the critical things wrong. In contrast, an awkward and unconventional swing may in fact be a solid one because it gets all the key elements right. The devil is in the details and we must know where to look. In some occasions, we even have to rely on recording instruments to see those fine details.

At first glance, an iron swing and a driver swing might look similar or nearly identical. But under the hood they have subtle yet crucial differences and require two different sets of swing thoughts to execute. Understanding the main differences between the two swings can save beginners a lot of headache and frustration. The sooner they come to realize these, the faster they can improve. I really wish someone had given me a lesson on this topic during my first year of playing the game. Keep in mind, this chapter is just a quick rundown of the key aspects. Golfers are encouraged to do more research in this area.

THE IRON SWING

To be a good iron player, one must be able to make solid contact when a ball is sitting directly on the ground. This is quite different compared to hitting a drive, in which the ball is on a tee with plenty of clearance. The margin for error is much smaller in an iron shot, especially when the ball is on a tight lie, and it takes good mind-body coordination to catch the ball clean and solid.

Setup and Ball Position

The setup posture for an iron shot is relatively neutral and no drastic upper body tilt is recommended. The ball is usually placed near the middle of the stance but can be moved forward or backward slightly based on the club used and the type of shot the golfer wants to hit (Fig. 12-1). For example, to hit a low shot, the ball can be moved toward the right foot.

Fig. 12-1 Setup for an Iron Shot

Hitting Down on the Ball

One of the key characteristics of a solid iron shot is that the club strikes the ball with a downward motion. The clubhead makes contact with the ball before it touches the ground (Fig. 12-2). This motion can be evidenced by the target-side divots left by good ball strikers in their iron shots. These demonstrate that the bottom of the swing arc is not under the ball but a few inches on the target side.

If you want to assess the iron skill of a fellow golfer, simply pay attention to the location of his divots. Someone who can take target-side divots consistently won't be a lousy iron player.

Fig. 12-2 Hitting Down with an Iron

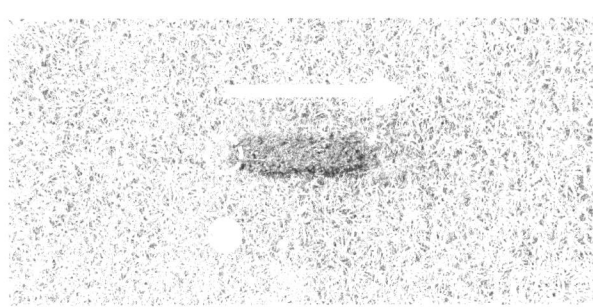

Fig. 12-3 Target Side Divot

Hitting down in an iron shot offers multiple advantages or benefits. One benefit is the ability to maximize ball speed. When a club approaches a ball at a very shallow attack angle and along a path that is quite close to the ground, it can easily catch obstacles, such as grasses, debris, and dirt, before contacting the ball. These obstacles not only slow down the clubhead but also contaminate the clubface, both of which are detrimental to the quality of a shot.

By attacking a ball along a downward path, the clubhead will approach the ball with greater ground clearance and have a much better chance of avoiding those obstacles. The clubhead will able to strike a ball cleanly with a higher speed. By the time the club touches the ground and slows down, the ball is already in the air.

Hitting down, which is often accompanied by a forward-leaning shaft, also facilitates making solid contact. When attacking the ball with a downward motion, the sweet spot of the clubface is better exposed to the ball. A golfer who takes a flat swing near impact could consciously lift the club to avoid ground obstacles, and fail to catch the ball on the sweet spot of the clubface.

Generally, golfers should consider hitting down when a ball is on the ground to increase the chance of making solid contact unless the lie is unusual and needs special treatments. This guideline not only applies to irons, but also to hybrids and fairway woods.

The sweet spot on a fairway wood or hybrid is relatively low and can be accessed easily. That is one of the reasons why a 4-hybrid is much easier to hit than a 4-iron. With the ball on a good lie, these clubs can make solid contact even with a flat sweeping motion. However, hitting down slightly is still a better option because the club can better avoid making pre-impact contact with obstacles and losing clubhead speed. Keep in mind however, hitting down with these clubs at too steep an attack angle can produce too much backspin, which can cause the ball to rise too high in the air and lose distance.

Hitting down is optional when a ball is on a tee, because the club now has a much better chance of catching the ball on the sweet spot. In this case, it is perfectly acceptable to sweep the club at impact, or even hit up slightly if you need a higher launch angle.

Jack Nicklaus talked about sweeping long irons with a driver swing in his book *My Golden Lessons*. He would catch the ball just a fraction of an inch before the clubhead reaches the swing bottom.

Tiger Woods also has made a similar statement in his book *How I Play Golf*. He would always tee the ball up when playing par-3 holes. For long irons, he would tee the ball half an inch above the ground and strike it with a sweep motion. With mid and short irons, he would tee the ball barely above the turf and hit down on it.

Forward-leaning Shaft at Impact

Another key attribute of a good iron shot is a forward leaning shaft at the moment of impact (Fig. 12-4). This is not only the case for full iron shots but also true for pitching and even chipping. Take a close look at a PGA tour player's iron swing in slow-motion, and you will see just that.

A forward-leaning shaft facilitates the hitting down motion and gives the clubhead a better chance to catch the ball clean and solid. It also lowers the effective loft and allows a ball to launch lower and travel farther.

Fig. 12-4 Forward-leaning Shaft

From the anatomic perspective, a forward-leaning shaft is usually accompanied by a bowed left wrist, which offers stronger and sturdier support in high-speed ball striking. A bowed left wrist also makes it possible to keep the clubface square for a longer duration around impact.

Many average golfers probably may not even realize that their shafts are in the neutral position at impact. The best way to check this is capturing the swing with a high frame rate (240 fps or higher) video camera.

The shaft lean might not be something that can be achieved instantly through conscious control. It is the result of proper swing motion and may take a lot of practice to accomplish.

In my opinion, the forward-leaning shaft position is closely associated with the swing lag, a challenging subject in golf swing. Swing lag keeps the hands ahead of the clubhead until ball striking is finished. If one tends to release the club too early, getting the shaft leaning forward can be difficult to do. Once you learn to maintain the lag in the downswing, the shaft leaning will come naturally.

Covering the Ball

In a good iron shot, a golfer's body should "cover the ball" at impact, meaning his chest should be right above the ball from the face-on view as if he was trying to keep the ball in his shadow (Fig. 12-4).

This posture allows the body to stay dynamically balanced and makes it easier to control the bottom of the swing arc and to deliver a powerful downward strike. Obviously, it is more difficult to hit a clean full iron shot with the chest falling behind or rushing ahead of the ball at impact.

How to Increase Spin Rate

Strong backspin is desirable in most approach shots since it helps distance control by limiting a ball's forward rolling power. There are a few things that can help increase the spin rate in an iron shot.
- Use urethane-covered premium balls.
- Make solid contact.
- Increase swing speed.
- Hit down on the ball to increase spin loft.
- Use a club with higher loft. A full swing with a higher-loft iron creates more spin than a partial swing with a lower-loft one.
- Open the clubface to further increase spin loft.
- Make sure the grooves are in good shape and free of debris.
- Wipe the clubface clean and dry before hitting a shot.

THE DRIVER SWING

Setup and Ball Position

The setup for a drive is different from that for an iron shot in many aspects. The stance for a drive is usually wider in order to provide a stable foundation for the high swing speed. The ball position is closer to the left foot, approximately in line with the golfer's inner left heel, as shown in Fig. 12-5. This facilitates ball striking on the upward swing arc.

The golfer's upper body typically tilts slightly away from the target with the sternum staying behind the ball to promote upward ball striking.

Fig. 12-5 Setup for a Drive

Neutral Shaft Position at Impact

In a good driver swing, the shaft is usually in a neutral position at impact. It may even tilts backward a little but barely leans toward the target as in an iron swing.

At impact, the golfer's head and sternum should all stay behind the ball to promote and support the upward strike (Fig. 12-6).

Fig. 12-6 Driver Shaft at Impact

Hitting Up

One important attribute of a good driver swing is *striking the ball on the upswing arc*. This is opposite to the approach used in an iron swing. With the ball on a tee and above the ground, the sweet spot of the driver can reach the ball easily. Ground obstacles are no longer a concern here. Thus there is no need to hit down in a tee shot with a driver.

According to real-world data, to get maximum driving distance golfers should limit ball spin and increase launch angle, which is the "high launch low spin" formula circulated within the golf community in recent years. It has been a recognized practice to swing a driver so that it catches the ball on the upswing arc, as seen in Fig. 12-7. This approach reduces spin loft and has been confirmed by launch monitors to produce a lower spin rate, a higher launch angle, and ultimately a longer driving distance.

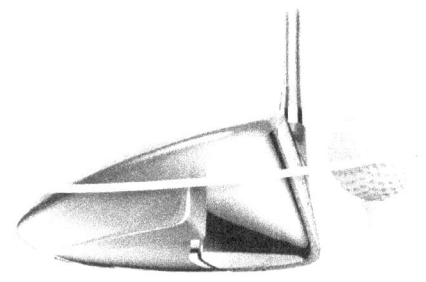

Fig. 12-7 Hitting up with a Driver

High Launch and Low Spin

Both scientific simulation and actual ball flight data have revealed that the combination of a reasonably high launch angle and a low spin rate is the recipe for longer driving distance. The concept of high launch and low spin has been a very popular topic among golfers. First, let's look at Table 12-1, which lists the ball flight data captured by a launch monitor.

Table 12-1

Data	Shot 1	Shot 2
Club Speed	90	90
Dynamic Loft	8.1	18.1
Attack Angle	-5	+5
Launch Angle	11.1	16.4
Spin Rate	3690	2630
Carry Distance	191	214

With the same clubhead speed, the second shot gained 23 yards in carry distance simply by changing the attack angle from -5° to +5°, which creates a higher launch angle and a lower spin rate.

With the same spin rate, a higher ball speed will generate a stronger lift. Since the ball speed in a drive is very high, we only need a moderate spin rate to produce the lift needed to fight gravity. In fact, too high a spin rate is detrimental because the lift will overpower gravity and cause a ball to rise too high in the air and lose distance (Fig. 12-8). We appreciate backspin in golf, but certainly don't want too much of it in a drive.

According to research data, the ideal launch angle for maximum distance is 10~16°, depending on the specific clubhead speed and spin rate. A driver with a higher loft can also produce a higher launch angle, but it would also create a higher backspin rate. To increase launch angle and keep the spin rate low, the right approach is to strike a ball on the upswing.

According to the data provided by TrackMan, the average drive attack angle among PGA tour players is -1.2°. However, most of the long shooters on the tour have a positive attack angle with their drivers.

Justin Thomas:	+4.5
Dustin Johnson:	+3.0
Rory McIlroy:	+2.2~2.5
Jon Rahm:	+2.0
Jason Day:	+1.2~2

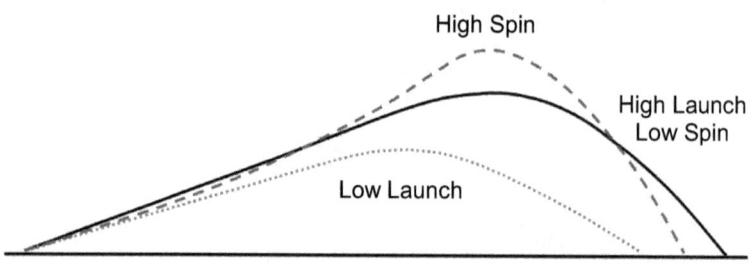

Fig. 12-8 Drive Trajectories

If you don't want to hit the ball too high in a drive, the least you should do is to sweep the ball horizontally at impact. Don't hit down with a driver unless you are "hitting off the deck," which means hitting a driver on the fairway with the ball on the ground.

The ideal spin rate in a drive should be 2000~3000 rpm, depending on the ball speed. The average drive spin rate for PGA tour players is 2686 rpm, but long shooters like Dustin Johnson likes to keep it around 2200 rpm. An amateur should have his swing and driver checked if he is getting a spin rate of 3500 rpm or higher.

How to Reduce Spin Rate in a Drive

Too high a spin rate is not desirable in a drive if the goal is to maximize distance and keep the ball in the fairway. There are several ways to bring down the spin rate in a drive to boost distance.

- Tee a ball higher and strike it on the upswing arc to reduce spin loft.
- Catch the ball slightly above the sweet spot on a driver's clubface and use vertical gear effect to reduce backspin.
- Choose low compression soft balls that feature low spin for driver shots.
- Apply lubricant on the clubface (illegal in competitions).
- Use a driver with a lower loft angle. This will reduce backspin but will also increase the influence of the sidespin.

Glossary

Angle of Attack

Angle of attack, or attack angle, refers to the angle between clubhead velocity (or club moving direction) and the leveled ground at the moment of maximum ball compression during impact. Typically the attack angle of a downward strike is defined as negative, whereas that of an upward strike is positive.

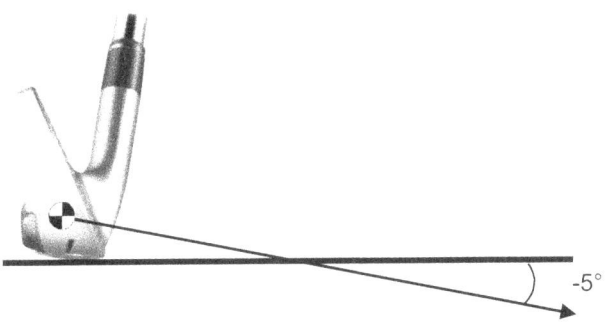

Fig. G-1 Angle of Attack

Ball Speed

Ball speed usually refers to a ball's launch speed when discussing ball striking. It measures how fast a ball travels immediately after impact. It is the primary factor that determines carry distance.

Carry Distance

Carry distance is the straight line ground level distance a golf ball travels from impact to its first landing. The carry distance provided by launch monitors is not directly measured. Instead, it is calculated based on the assumption that the landing location is at the same elevation level as the launch location.

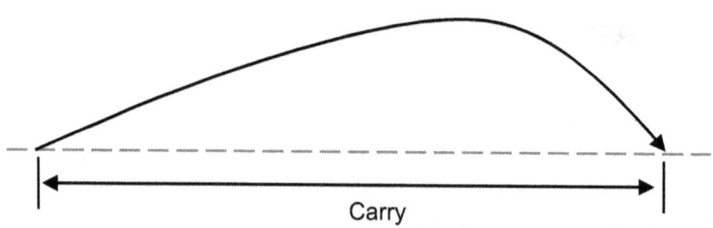

Fig. G-2 Carry Distance

Clubhead Speed

Clubhead speed, also called swing speed or club speed, measures how fast the center of the clubface travels right before impact. Clubhead speed is the key factor that determines ball speed.

COR

COR stands for *Coefficient of Restitution*. It is used to measure how much kinetic energy is sustained in a collision between two objects. It is the ratio of the relative speed of two objects after impact to the relative speed before impact.

If COR equals one then no kinetic energy is lost in the collision, which is known as an elastic collision. A COR of 0.83, which is the limit stipulated by the USGA, means 17% of the kinetic energy is lost and the collision is inelastic.

DYNAMIC LOFT

It is the same as *Effective Loft*.

EFFECTIVE LOFT

Effective loft refers to the angle between clubface normal and ground plane at impact. For an iron, the effective loft is the same for the entire clubface; for a driver or fairway wood, it should be measured at the center of the impact location. A ball's launch angle is mainly determined by the effective loft. A golfer can decrease the effective loft, and consequently the launch angle, by leaning the shaft forward at impact. In a radar-based launch monitor, effective loft is not directly measured but calculated using a model.

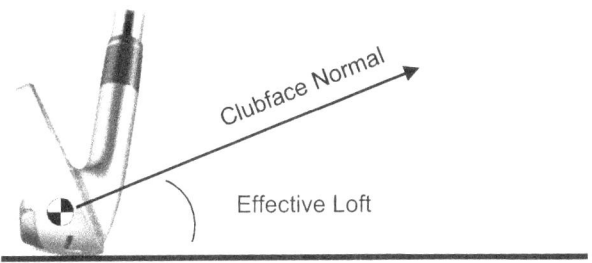

Fig. G-3 Effective Loft

FACE ANGLE

Face angle is the angle between the target line and the Y-plane (or the ground projection of the clubface normal). A positive angle means the clubface points to the right of the target line (i.e., clubface is open to the target line). A negative number means the clubface points to the left of the target line (clubface is closed). A ball's launch direction is mainly determined the face angle.

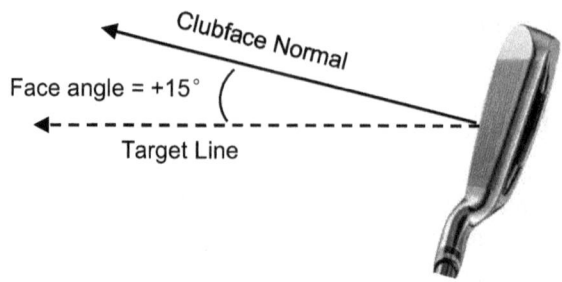

Fig. G-4 Face Angle

DRAW

Draw is a ball flight that curves in the direction opposite to the golfer's dominant hand. For right-handed golfers, a draw curves moderately from right to left.

FADE

Fade is a ball flight that curves in the direction of the golfer's dominant hand. For right-handed golfers, a fade curves moderately from left to right.

FACE-TO-PATH

Face-to-path is a term that TrackMan uses to describe the angle between the swing path and the clubface orientation at. The angle is positive if the clubface is open to the swing path; or negative if the clubface is closed to it. At impact, this angle determines the magnitude of sidespin and can be considered the sidespin loft.

Hook

Hook is a ball flight that drastically curves in the direction opposite to the golfer's dominant hand. For right-handed golfers, the ball flight of a hook curves severely from right to left.

Horizontal Launch Angle

It is the same as *Launch Direction*, but technically more accurate.

Horizontal Swing Direction

Horizontal swing direction is a clubhead's moving direction seen from the bird's eye view. Technically it is the projection of clubhead velocity on a horizontal plane at the moment of impact. It usually uses the target line as the reference.

Landing Angle

Landing angle is the angle a ball approaches its first landing point. Landing angle affects how far a ball can roll after hitting the ground. For drives, a narrower landing angle is favorable for rolling distance. For approach shots, a greater landing angle allows a ball to stop sooner.

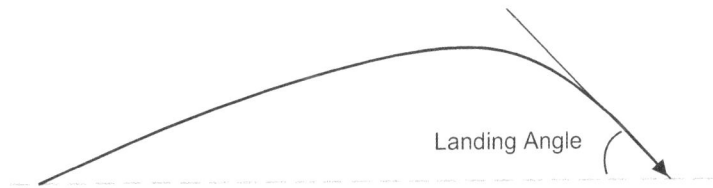

Fig. G-5 Landing Angle

LAUNCH ANGLE

Launch angle is the angle between a ball's travel direction and the ground plane immediately after impact. It is also called *Vertical Launch Angle*.

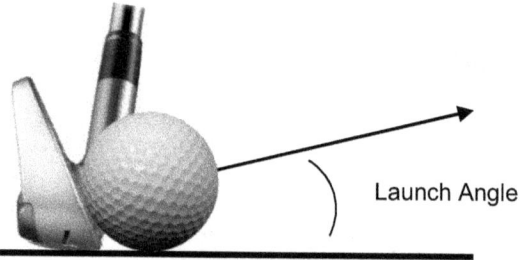

Fig. G-6 Launch Angle

LAUNCH DIRECTION

Launch direction, also called *Horizontal Launch Angle*, is the angle between the ground projection of ball velocity and the target line immediately after impact. For leading launch monitors, a positive angle means the launch direction points to the right of the target line; whereas a negative angle means the launch direction points to the left of the target line.

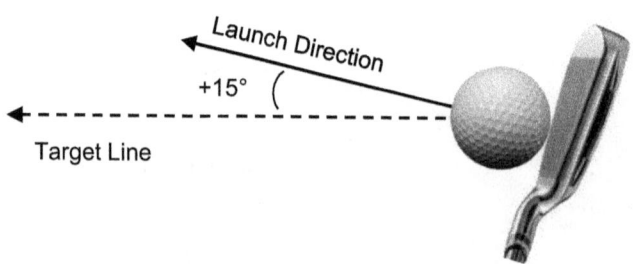

Fig. G-7 Launch Direction

Launch Monitor

An electronic device used to measure a ball's launch parameters, including ball speed, club speed, spin rate, launch angle, launch direction, etc. It also offers calculated data, such as distance, face angle, impact location etc., using mathematic modeling.

Launch Vector

Launch Vector is a term used in this book. The clubhead velocity can be decomposed into two components. The component in the clubface normal direction is called the launch vector since it is primary function is to launch a ball into the air.

Moment of Inertia, MOI

Moment of Inertia (MOI) is an attribute that describes an object's tendency to resist angular acceleration. A club with higher MOI will show more resistance to rotation under a specific torque, and is therefore more forgiving to off-center shots.

Offset Distance

Offset distance measures how much a ball drifts sideways from the target line. It is the shortest distance between a ball's final landing location and the target line.

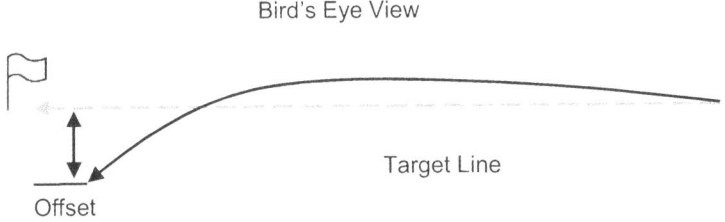

Fig. G-8 Offset Distance

Pull

For a right-handed golfer, a pull is a straight shot launched toward the left of the target. For a left-handed golfer, it is a straight shot launched toward the right of the target.

Push

For a right-handed golfer, a push is a straight shot launched toward the right of the target. For a left-handed golfer, a push is a straight shot launched toward the left of the target.

Neutral Shaft Position

When in the neutral position, a shaft is perpendicular to the target line and appears to be perpendicular to the ground from a face-on view. The shaft doesn't lean toward or away from the target.

Slice

A slice is a ball flight drastically curves in the direction of the player's dominant hand. For right-handed golfers, the ball flight curves severely from left to right.

Smash Factor

Smash factor is an indicator of relative shot quality. It is defined as the ratio of the ball speed right after impact to the clubhead speed prior to impact.

Smash Factor = Ball Speed / Clubhead Speed

Spin Axis

Spin axis is the axis around which a golf ball spins. For many launch monitors, a spin axis tilting clockwise is designated with a positive angle. In contrast, a spin axis tilting counterclockwise has a negative value. The direction of spin axis follows the right-hand rule: with the curled long fingers matching the spin direction, the straight thumb represents the direction of the spin axis.

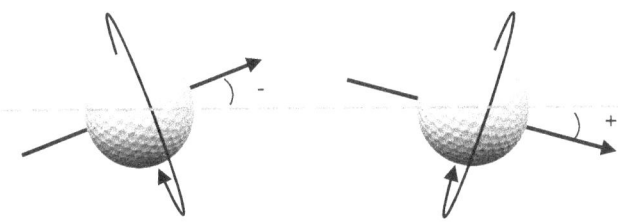

Fig. G-9 Spin Axis

Spinning Vector

The clubhead velocity can be decomposed into two components. The velocity component parallel to the clubface is called the spinning vector in this book since it is responsible for producing spin.

Spin Loft

Spin loft is the angle between the clubface normal and the clubhead velocity (or clubhead swing direction) at impact. For a driver, the spin loft is measured at the actual impact location. Spin loft determines the relative strength of the spinning vector. For a given clubhead speed, a higher spin loft produces a greater spinning vector, which usually results in a higher spin rate.

Spin Rate

Spin rate measures how fast a golf ball rotates around its own axis immediately after impact. Typically, a club with a greater loft angle produces higher spin rates. A sand wedge can produce a spin rate exceeding 10,000 rpm whereas a driver's typical spin rate is only 2000~3000 rpm.

Striking Plane

Striking plane is the plane on which the club shaft should travel near impact in order to produce solid and consistent shots. A club only travels on this plane when it is below the waist of the golfer during downswing. See *Decoding the Golf Swing Plane* for more details.

Swing Path

Swing path is a collection of positions that a clubhead's CG passes during its movement. Swing path is really a 3D concept but people often talk about its 2D projection on the ground plane.

What really matters to ball flight is the clubhead's velocity or swing direction, which is tangential to the swing path at any point.

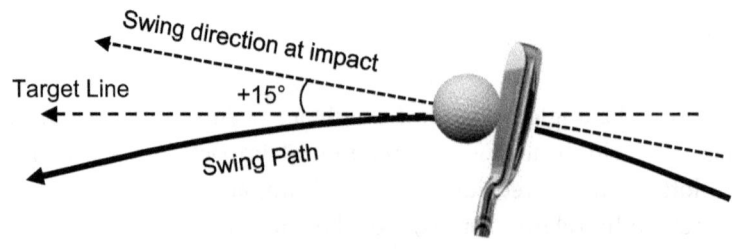

Fig. G-10 Swing Path

Swing Direction

Swing direction indicates where the clubhead is moving at a certain point of time. It is the direction where the clubhead velocity points to at that moment. When a clubhead is moving along a circular arc, its swing direction (and direction of its velocity) at any point is the tangential direction of the arc.

Swing Plane Angle

Swing plane angle refers to the angle between the swing plane and the ground. In some launch monitors, this is referred to as Swing Plane or Vertical Swing Plane.

Target Line

Target line is an imaginary straight line connecting the ball and the intended target at setup.

Total Distance

Total distance is the straight line ground distance from impact to a ball's final stop. The total distance given by a launch monitor is not an actual measurement but a calculated value.

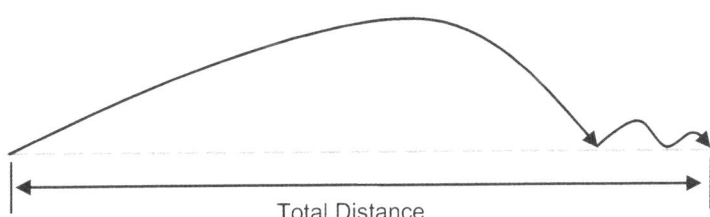

Fig. G-11 Total Distance

VERTICAL LAUNCH ANGLE

It is the same as *Launch Angle*.

Y-PLANE

Y-plane is an imaginary plane that is perpendicular to the grooves and also passes the CG of the clubhead. It is used to indicate the orientation of the clubface. A clubface is square to the target line when the Y-plane is perpendicular to the ground and contains the target line, no matter how the effective loft changes.

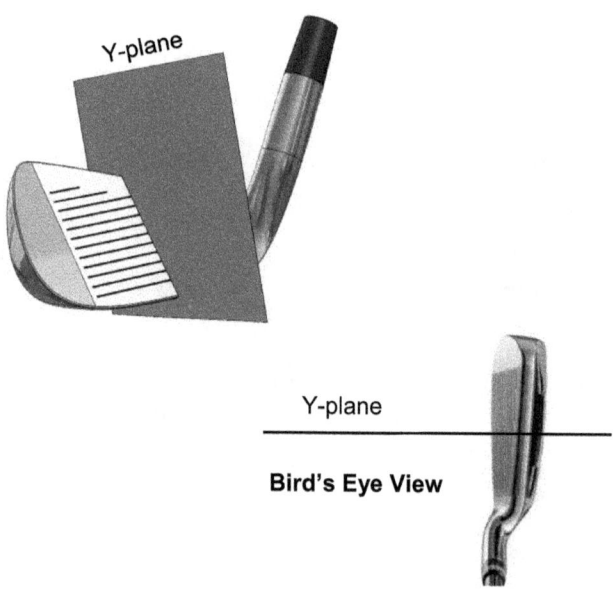

Fig. G-12 The Y-Plane

About the Author

Xichao Mo graduated from Nankai University with a Master's degree in Electrical Engineering. He is now a senior electrical engineer and an entrepreneur. As an avid amateur golfer who enjoys studying golf swing theories and ball striking techniques, Xichao has published several Amazon best-selling books.

His book *Decoding the Golf Swing Plane*, which debunks the myths and reveals the ultimate truths of golf swing plane, is the first book ever dedicated to this important subject in the game of golf. Since its release in 2014, *Decoding the Golf Swing Plane* has received great reviews from renowned PGA teaching professionals as well as golf enthusiasts. It has been one of the bestselling golf books on Amazon and was featured in Martin Hall's School of Golf on Golf Channel in September, 2014.

Your opinions and comments are always welcome.
Emails: maxgolf@outlook.com
www.golfswingtraining.com

Decoding the Golf Swing Plane

- An Amazon Best-selling Golf Book
- Featured on Golf Channel
- Recommended by PGA Teaching Pros
- A Must-read for Avid Golfers

Book Reviews

I haven't seen anything more thoroughly researched, more accurate and more advanced on the specific subject of how the swing plane actually works. If you're interested in this sort of thing, this book is an absolute must-have.

Stephen Finley

I have not had a golf book that I literally read at a go like this one. Incredible analysis and very clear explanations for the swing. It thoroughly explains why very "different" looking postures still present same results. The Book requires very good understanding of angles and a bit of very simple physics. It is written for the analytical minds more than anything else. It will open your eyes to certain things you have been doing wrong.

Amazon Review

The authors explain in great detail just what defines the golf swing plane, how to find it, and how to stay on it. I found the book to be very readable throughout, but I would caution that this book is for golfers who enjoy great detail. This is not a casual glance at the topic of swing plane. It is a book that will stay on my tablet.

Amazon Review

It offers a good explanation of how to get the club into the hitting zone. Although highly technical, I think most golfers who have been at it for a few years will appreciate the detailed explanation.

Clayton W. Beeson

This is an enjoyable book with a sensible concept. I really like the concept of translating a "flat" swing to a "tilted" swing plane.

Paul D. Ross

Fabulous book! This book will help you understand the essence of the golf swing. It will help you better understand the ideas of Jim Hardy. This book presents the essential concept of having the club on plane, but only when the club is below waist high on the "striking plane." All good players do this. Jim Furyk, Fred Couples, Bubba, Tiger, Jack ... they all look the same coming into impact, with the club shaft on the striking plane. A great read.

Dan Leonard

It increased my understanding of the swing plane. Glad I bought it and recommend it to others.

Terry B.

From what I've read Mr. Hogan expected someone in the future to improve on his teachings. Well this is it. Finally a description of the swing plane that is understandable and makes scientific sense. Well done!

Dennis J. McMahon

A necessary read for any serious student of the game.

Billy H.

This is a great read for golfers of all levels. I've read many books on the golf swing, and this one is a winner. Hope every golfer finds this book

Amazon Review

What any serious student of golf will see immediately is the originality. Trust me when I tell you, it is something you HAVE NOT read before. This book helped me immediately. The upright swing examinations solidify his unique insight and ingenuity. After reading it well, you will want to refer to it daily. Great book!

Amazon Review

This is a must read for every golfer. Really surprised at how much the book helped me. Best $15.00 I ever spent on something to do with golf.

Michelle Thompson

This book is great for getting to the details of a golf swing from setup to follow thru. The book and diagrams reinforced my own understanding of the swing, and opened my eyes to a new understanding.

Amazon Review

The authors explain in great detail just what defines the golf swing plane, how to find it, and how to stay on it. I found the book to be very readable throughout, but I would caution that this book is for golfers who enjoy great detail. This is not a casual glance at the topic of swing plane. It is a book that will stay on my tablet.

Amazon Review

www.ingramcontent.com/pod-product-compliance
Lightning Source LLC
Chambersburg PA
CBHW071715090426
42738CB00009B/1783